Picture Atlas

A DORLING KINDERSLEY BOOK

LONDON, NEW YORK,
MELBOURNE, MUNICH, and DELHI

Authors Anita Ganeri and Chris Oxlade
Senior Editor Ben Morgan
Senior Art Editors Janet Allis, Cheryl Telfer
Editor Simon Holland
Additional design Jacqueline Gooden,
Mary Sandberg, Floyd Sayer, Sonia Whillock
Editorial Assistant Fleur Star
Digital Map Illustrator Peter Bull

Publishing Manager Sue Leonard
Managing Art Editor Clare Shedden
Jacket design Poppy Jenkins, Bob Warner
Picture Researchers Martin Copeland,
Sean Hunter, Sarah Stewart-Richardson
Production Controller Linda Dare
DTP Designer Almudena Díaz

This edition published in 2013.
First published in Great Britain in 2003 by
Dorling Kindersley Limited
80 Strand, London WC2R 0RL

Penguin Group (UK)
10 9 8 7 6 5 4 3 2 1
001–DD041–Jun/13

A catalogue record for this book
is available from the British Library.

ISBN 978-1-4093-4154-3

Colour reproduction by Colourscan, Singapore
Printed and bound in China by
South China Printing Company Ltd.

discover more at
www.dk.com

Contents

Our world

The top of the world

The Americas

Our world

Land covers a third of planet Earth, and water and ice cover the rest. We divide the land into seven main chunks called continents. The sea is divided in five major areas called oceans.

North America

Atlantic Ocean

Pacific Ocean

Inside the Earth

The inside of Earth is made of hot, molten rock that slowly swirls about like thick treacle. We live on a thin, solid crust, a bit like the crust of a pie.

South America

Where people live

This picture of Earth at night was taken by a satellite in space. The bright bits are made by lights on the surface. They show where the world's big cities and towns are.

4

How long would a trip around the Equator take at walking speed?

Arctic Ocean

Europe

Asia

Pacific
Ocean

Africa

Equator

Indian
Ocean

Australia

The Equator is
an imaginary line
around the middle
of the world.

The Southern Ocean runs all the way around Antarctica.

Southern Ocean

Antarctica

Seven continents

North America, South America, Europe,
Asia, Africa, Australia, and Antarctica are
Earth's continents. Sometimes people call
Europe and Asia one continent (Eurasia).

Can you find...

The smallest continent?
The continent of Australia is
also the world's biggest island.

**The most crowded
continent?** About 3,500
million people live in Asia.

The biggest ocean? The
Pacific Ocean is as big as all
other oceans put together.

About a year (without stopping for a rest).

5

Maps and atlases

A map is a drawing of the ground that shows where towns, rivers, and other important features lie. An atlas is a book of maps.

Making a flat map of the world is like peeling an orange.

Thin areas need to be stretched to make a full rectangle.

Peeling the Earth
Earth is ball-shaped, so a globe is the best kind of map to show the whole planet. On a flat map, some areas are stretched or squashed.

How to use this book
This atlas is divided into map pages and information pages. The key tells you what the map symbols mean.

Key to maps

- ◉ CAPITAL CITY
- ● State capital
- • Town
- ▲ Mountain
- • • • Key feature
- ⌒ Border
- - - - State border
- ⌒ River

Compass points show you which way is north, south, east, and west.

Small pictures show the things you might see if you visited the country, from famous buildings to native animals and national sports.

Atlas questions test your general knowledge about different parts of the world. The answer is upside down on the opposite page.

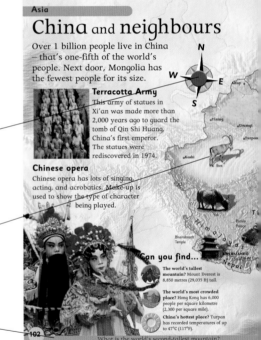

Asia

China and neighbours

Over 1 billion people live in China — that's one-fifth of the world's people. Next door, Mongolia has the fewest people for its size.

Terracotta Army
This army of statues in Xi'an was made more than 2,000 years ago to guard the tomb of Qin Shi Huang, China's first emperor. The statues were rediscovered in 1974.

Chinese opera
Chinese opera has lots of singing, acting, and acrobatics. Make-up is used to show the type of character being played.

Can you find...

The world's tallest mountain? Mount Everest is 8,850 metres (29,035 ft) tall.

The world's most crowded place? Hong Kong has 6,000 people per square kilometre (2,300 per square mile).

China's hottest place? Turpan has recorded temperatures of up to 47°C (117°F).

What is the world's second-tallest mountain?

Earth's landscapes
The background patterns on the maps show what the landscape and countryside are like in different parts of the world.

Deciduous forest
Forests of trees that lose their leaves in autumn.

Grassland
Flat, grassy plains with a few trees dotted about.

Coniferous forest
Forests of conifer trees, which are green all year round.

What sort of map shows just countries and their borders?

Types of maps

People use different kinds of maps for different purposes. Road maps help drivers find the way. In cities, people on foot use street maps.

Road maps show routes between towns and cities.

Get going

To find out why world maps are stretched, peel an orange and see if you make a rectangle with the skin. Does it help if you cut the skin into thin strips?

A tube map of London shows underground train stations and the tracks between them.

A street map shows city streets and buildings.

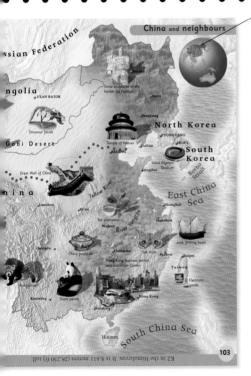

Globes show where the map is on Earth's surface. The featured countries are highlighted in red.

Buttons contain a file of facts about special topics, such as local animals or foods.

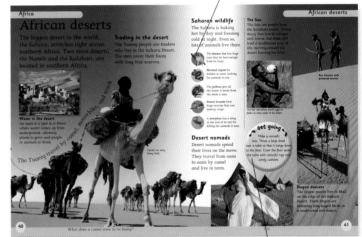

Information pages

After each map are information pages, which are packed with amazing facts about the countries in the map.

Get going circles contain great ideas for projects and experiments you can carry out.

Desert
Dry sand and rock with hardly any plants.

Rainforest
A jungle of tall trees and layers of thick undergrowth.

Snow and ice
High in the mountains and near the poles.

Mountains
Rugged landscape of tall hills and valleys, often snow covered.

Oceans
Seas and oceans cover two-thirds of the Earth.

A political map.

World climates

Near the Earth's poles, it is freezing cold all year round. But near the Equator it is always hot and rainy. We say that the poles and Equator have different climates.

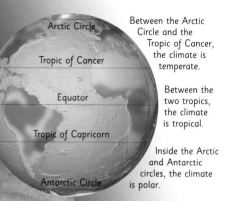

Arctic Circle

Tropic of Cancer

Equator

Tropic of Capricorn

Antarctic Circle

Between the Arctic Circle and the Tropic of Cancer, the climate is temperate.

Between the two tropics, the climate is tropical.

Inside the Arctic and Antarctic circles, the climate is polar.

Climate zones

World maps show horizontal lines that divide Earth into zones with different climates. Tropical zones are always warm and polar zones are always cold. Temperate zones are a mixture of the two, with warm summers and cool winters.

Polar climate

Antarctica has a polar climate. It is always freezing cold, and there are fierce blizzards. Penguins keep warm by growing a thick layer of fat and huddling together.

Conifer forest

In some parts of the temperate zones, winters are long and cold, so conifers are the only trees that survive. Some flowers appear in the short summers.

Emperor penguins

What's another name for tropical grassland?

Desert

A desert climate is very dry all year round. Deserts can be baking hot in the day but very cold at night.

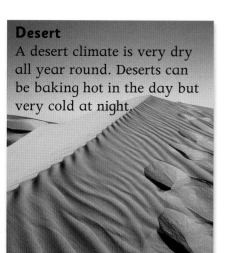

Toucans live in tropical rainforest. They have huge beaks for eating tropical fruits.

Tropical forest

Places near the Equator are both warm and rainy all year. Dense tropical rainforests grow here.

Tropical grassland

Some tropical places have a dry season and a rainy season every year. Trees are less common here, and the ground is covered with grass.

Deciduous trees change colour as their leaves die in autumn.

Deciduous forest

Warmer parts of the temperate zone are full of trees that shed their leaves in winter. We call them deciduous trees.

Maple leaves

Poison dart frog

Seas and oceans

Seas and oceans cover about two-thirds of the world. Beneath the surface they are full of life. Most sea creatures live in habitats near the coast, such as coral reefs. But there is also life far out in the open ocean and on the deep sea floor.

Dolphins

Shark

Sperm whale

Giant squid

Most animals and plants live in the sunlit surface waters near the coast.

Deeper down, the water is cold and gloomy.

No light reaches the deep sea. It is pitch black here.

Ocean waves

Waves are caused by wind blowing across the sea. When they reach shallow water they tumble over and turn into breakers.

Under the sea

Away from the shore, the land slopes steeply into the sea. Some of the seabed is covered in flat plains, but there are also mountains and valleys.

Animals of the deep

Some very strange animals live in the deep sea. The gulper eel lives 7 km (4 miles) down and catches dead creatures as they sink from above. Its mouth is so huge it can swallow animals bigger than itself.

What is the deepest place in the world's oceans?

The open ocean

Out in the open ocean there is less life than near the coast. Occasional shoals of fish are food for big animals, such as dolphins.

Dolphins sometimes drive fish into tight balls before attacking them.

Kelp forests

This seaweed is called giant kelp. It grows from the seabed, making thick forests where fish and other animals live.

Angel fish

Life on the coast

Animals and plants that live on the shore are battered by the waves. They cling to rocks or burrow into sandy beaches.

Tentacle of a sea cucumber (an animal related to a starfish).

Coral reefs

Coral reefs are home to thousands of different sea creatures, including many colourful fish. Reefs grow slowly in shallow tropical seas and are made up of the hard cases of tiny animals (corals).

The Mariana Trench in the Pacific Ocean. It is 11 km (6.9 miles) deep.

The Arctic

At the top of the world is the North Pole, and around this is an area called the Arctic. The Arctic is mostly ocean. In its centre is a gigantic lump of floating ice that never completely melts. Further out are the northern tips of the continents and the huge island of Greenland.

Arctic people

Arctic people live in the icy lands around the Arctic Ocean. The weather is too cold for growing crops, so Arctic people get all their food from animals. They survive by fishing, herding reindeer, and hunting seals and whales.

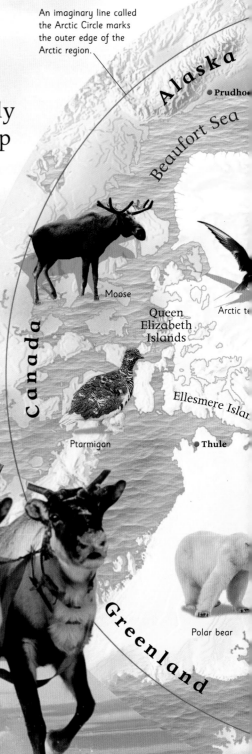

An imaginary line called the Arctic Circle marks the outer edge of the Arctic region.

Alaska

Prudho●

Beaufort Sea

Canada

Moose

Queen Elizabeth Islands

Arctic te

Ellesmere Islar

Ptarmigan

● Thule

Polar bear

Greenland

12

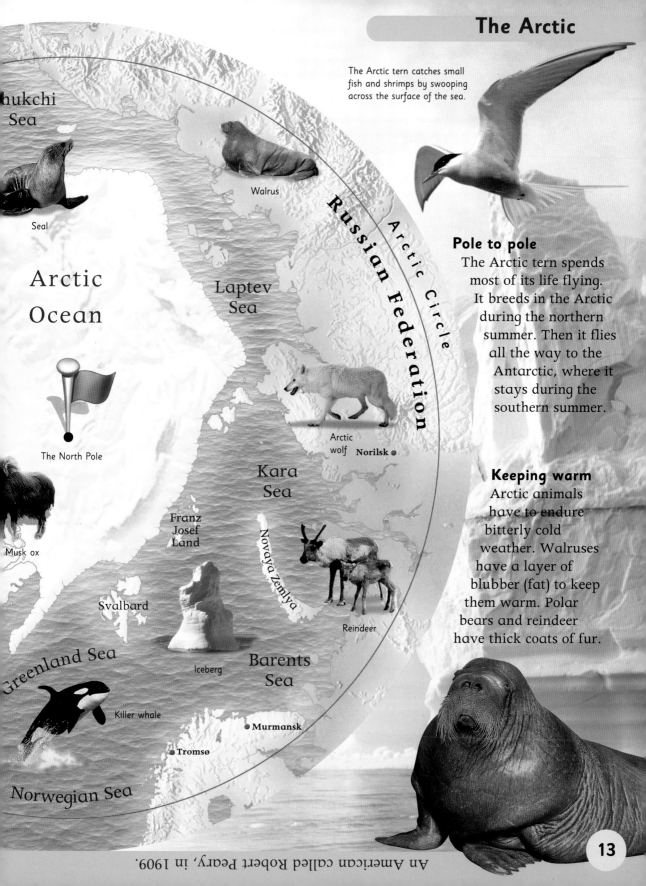

The Arctic

The Arctic tern catches small fish and shrimps by swooping across the surface of the sea.

Chukchi Sea

Seal

Walrus

Russian Federation

Arctic Circle

Pole to pole

The Arctic tern spends most of its life flying. It breeds in the Arctic during the northern summer. Then it flies all the way to the Antarctic, where it stays during the southern summer.

Arctic Ocean

Laptev Sea

Arctic wolf **Norilsk**

Keeping warm

Arctic animals have to endure bitterly cold weather. Walruses have a layer of blubber (fat) to keep them warm. Polar bears and reindeer have thick coats of fur.

The North Pole

Kara Sea

Musk ox

Franz Josef Land

Novaya Zemlya

Reindeer

Svalbard

Iceberg

Greenland Sea

Killer whale

Barents Sea

Murmansk

Tromsø

Norwegian Sea

13

An American called Robert Peary, in 1909.

The Arctic

The Arctic is a magical place, but it is also freezing cold and dangerous. For the people and animals that live there, life is very tough indeed.

Arctic travel

Arctic people have to travel across ice, snow, and the sea.

Snowshoes spread your weight to stop your feet sinking into snow.

Skidoos zoom over snow with motorised tracks and a steerable ski.

Kayaks are wooden canoes used by Inuit people for fishing.

Sledges carry heavy loads or people. They are pulled by dogs.

Northern lights

At night, the Arctic sky lights up with shimmering colours called the northern lights. They are caused by particles from space hitting Earth's atmosphere.

Thick fur clothes and fur-lined hoods keep out the cold.

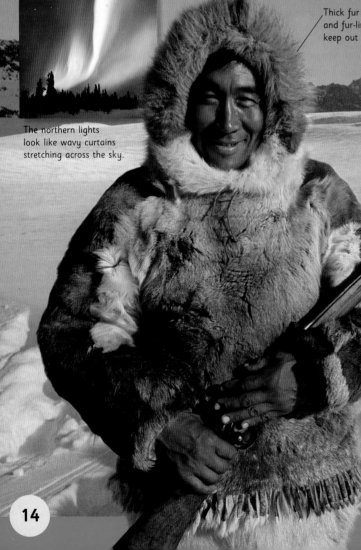

The northern lights look like wavy curtains stretching across the sky.

Rifles are used for hunting and to scare away polar bears.

Inuit hunters

The Inuit people live in Canada and Greenland. They use spears and guns to hunt seals, whales, fish, walruses, and polar bears.

Why is summer in the Arctic unusual?

Polar bear

The world's biggest and most deadly kind of bear is the polar bear, which lives in the Arctic. Polar bears mostly hunt seals, but they occasionally kill people too.

Igloos

Most Inuit people live in modern houses in small towns. On long hunting trips they sleep in igloos – temporary shelters made from blocks of snow.

Icebreakers

In winter the Arctic Ocean freezes solid. Special ships called icebreakers keep channels clear.

Husky dogs

Arctic people use teams of husky dogs to pull sledges. Huskies originally come from Siberia. They are very strong and have thicker fur than most dogs.

15

The Sun doesn't set.

Canada and Alaska

Canada is the second-largest country in the world, and Alaska is the largest of all the US states. Despite their huge size, both places have small populations, because much of the land is covered in thick forest or frozen for most of the year.

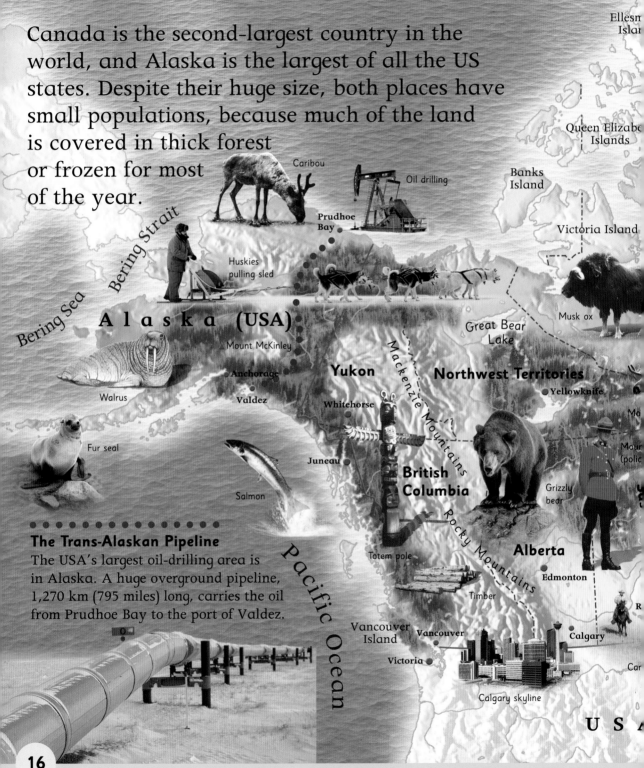

Ellesm
Islar

Queen Elizabe
Islands

Banks
Island

Victoria Island

Caribou

Oil drilling

Prudhoe
Bay

Musk ox

Huskies
pulling sled

Bering Strait

Bering Sea

A l a s k a   (USA)

Great Bear
Lake

Walrus

△ Mount McKinley

Yukon

Northwest Territories

• Yellowknife

Mo

Anchorage •

Mackenzie Mountains

Valdez •

Whitehorse •

Fur seal

Juneau •

**British
Columbia**

Grizzly
bear

Mour
(polic

Salmon

Rocky Mountains

Alberta

Totem pole

Edmonton •

Timber

R

Vancouver
Island

Vancouver •

Calgary •

Victoria •

Car

Calgary skyline

U S A

The Trans-Alaskan Pipeline

The USA's largest oil-drilling area is in Alaska. A huge overground pipeline, 1,270 km (795 miles) long, carries the oil from Prudhoe Bay to the port of Valdez.

Pacific Ocean

What is the tallest mountain in North America, at 6,194 m (20,320 ft) high?

Industries

Here are some of the main industries in the region.

Timber from trees is used as building material or for making furniture.

Oil is used to make fuels like petrol, and chemicals such as plastics.

Wheat is grown in the centre of Canada on prairies, which are huge, flat fields.

Metals such as zinc, aluminium, gold, and silver are mined in Canada.

N
E
W
S

Hooded seal

Baffin Island

Inuit children

Iqaluit

Canada goose

Right whales (whale watching is a popular activity)

havut

Black bear

Newfoundland and Labrador

Newfoundland dog

St. John's

n a d a

Hudson Bay

Beluga whale and calf

Mining

Gannet

Quebec

Prince Edward Island

Charlottetown

New Brunswick

Nova Scotia

Halifax

Quebec

Fredericton

Maple leaf

Beaver

Montreal

Snowboarding

CN Tower, Toronto

OTTAWA

Manitoba

Ontario

Winnipeg

Lake Superior

Lake Huron

Toronto

Lake Ontario

Lake Michigan

Lake Erie

Niagara Falls

Atlantic Ocean

Harbour porpoises

Canada and Alaska

Magnificent scenery and unspoilt wilderness make Canada and Alaska great places to live. However, the winters are long, dark, and bitterly cold. Most people live in the south, where the weather is mildest.

Alaskan landscape

The ten tallest mountains in the USA are all in Alaska. Mount McKinley (Denali) is the highest. Surrounding these huge mountains are forests and lakes.

Animal life

Despite the chilly weather, Canada, Alaska, and the surrounding sea are home to some spectacular animals.

Husky dogs are used to pull sleds that transport people and materials.

Walruses group together on Arctic beaches or floating sheets of ice.

Moose live in woods close to swamps, lakes, and other watery areas.

Right whales are sometimes hit by ships because they swim slowly.

Fur seals grow to about 2.1 m (7 ft) long. They eat fish and some birds.

Timber industry

Canada's trees can grow to enormous sizes, especially along the rainy west coast. Lumberjacks cut them down for timber (wood), which is used for building houses and making furniture.

18

What could you put on your pancakes to sweeten them?

Ice hockey

Thanks to the cold winters, Canadians can play ice hockey on outdoor rinks or frozen lakes and ponds. Ice hockey is the world's fastest team sport.

Native peoples

The Kwakiutl and Haida Indians were among the first people to live on Canada's west coast. They carved totem poles to tell stories about their families and traditions.

Totem pole

French Canadians

Europeans started coming to Canada in the 17th century, and many came from France. Today, most French Canadians live in the region called Quebec.

Hotel Chateau Frontenac, Quebec City, Quebec, Canada

CN Tower, Toronto

This is the world's tallest tower (but not the tallest building, since buildings have floors). It is 553 m (1,814 ft) high, which is taller than 300 people standing on each other's heads. A glass lift shoots up the outside to the main deck, which has a revolving restaurant and a scary glass floor.

Sweet treat

Maple syrup is made from the sap of maple trees. To make it, you drill a hole in a tree, collect the sap that dribbles out, and boil it until it thickens. Sugar maple trees produce the sweetest sap.

Canadian Pure
Maple Syrup
500 mL

Maple syrup.

United States of America

The United States of America is an enormous country made up of 50 states. There are mountains, deserts, forests, wetlands, and vast plains in the USA.

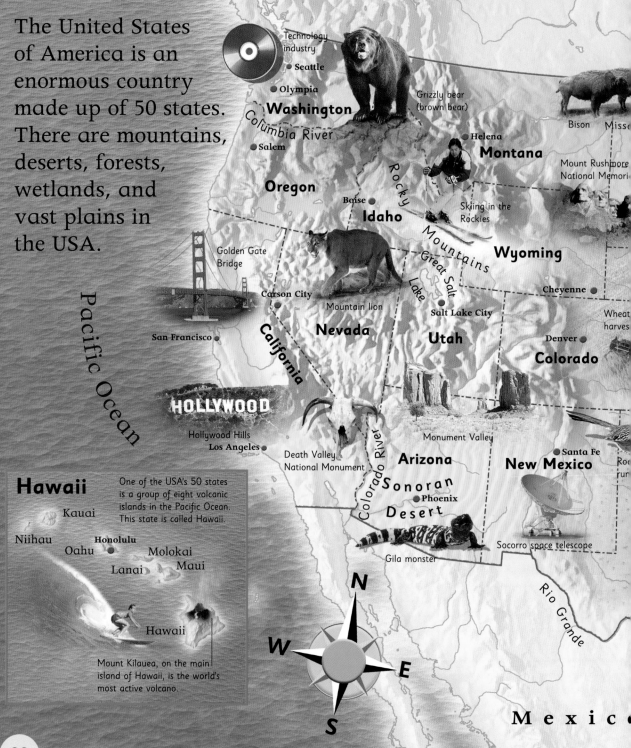

Technology industry

• Seattle

• Olympia

Washington

Columbia River

• Salem

Grizzly bear (brown bear)

Bison   Miss

• Helena

Montana

Mount Rushmore National Memori

Oregon

• Boise

Idaho

Rocky

Mountains

Skiing in the Rockies

Wyoming

Golden Gate Bridge

Mountain lion

Great Salt

Lake

• Cheyenne

Wheat harves

Carson City

Salt Lake City

Nevada

Utah

• Denver

Colorado

San Francisco

California

Pacific Ocean

HOLLYWOOD

Hollywood Hills

Los Angeles

Death Valley National Monument

Colorado River

Monument Valley

Arizona

Santa Fe

New Mexico

Roc

rur

Sonoran

• Phoenix

Desert

Socorro space telescope

Gila monster

Rio Grande

M e x i c o

Hawaii

One of the USA's 50 states is a group of eight volcanic islands in the Pacific Ocean. This state is called Hawaii.

Kauai

Niihau

Honolulu

Oahu

Molokai

Lanai

Maui

Hawaii

Mount Kilauea, on the main island of Hawaii, is the world's most active volcano.

N   W   E   S

Which is the only US state not shown on this map?

United States of America

This map shows 48 of the 50 states of the USA. The other two states are thousands of kilometres away. Alaska is northwest of Canada, and Hawaii is in the middle of the Pacific Ocean.

Canada

Lake Superior

Lake Huron

Lake Ontario

Lake Michigan

Lake Erie

North Dakota

ismarck

Minnesota

Wisconsin

Dairy farming

South Dakota

erre

Iowa

Nebraska

Lincoln

Raccoon

Michigan

Detroit

Chicago

Indiana

Illinois

Sears Tower, Chicago

St. Louis

American football

Ohio

New York

Statue of Liberty

Vermont

New Hampshire

Maine

Blueberries

Augusta

Massachusetts

Boston

Rhode Island

Connecticut

New York

New Jersey

Delaware

Pennsylvania

Harrisburg

Maryland

WASHINGTON DC

West Virginia

Virginia

The Capitol building, Washington, DC

Missouri

Topeka

Kansas

American bald eagle

Kentucky

Ohio River

Tennessee

Country music

Appalachian Mountains

Raleigh

North Carolina

South Carolina

Atlantic Ocean

Plains

Oklahoma City

"Tornado Alley"

Oklahoma

Arkansas

Little Rock

Mississippi River

Mississippi

Alabama

Montgomery

Atlanta

Georgia

Kennedy Space Center

Dallas

wells

Texas

Louisiana

Baton Rouge

New Orleans

Paddle steamer

Tallahassee

Florida

The Everglades

Dolphin-watching

Miami

Cowboy

Jazz music

American alligator

Gulf of Mexico

Alaska (see page 18).

21

United States of America

The USA is the world's richest and most powerful country. Many of the people live in huge, modern cities, yet there are still vast areas of unspoilt natural wilderness.

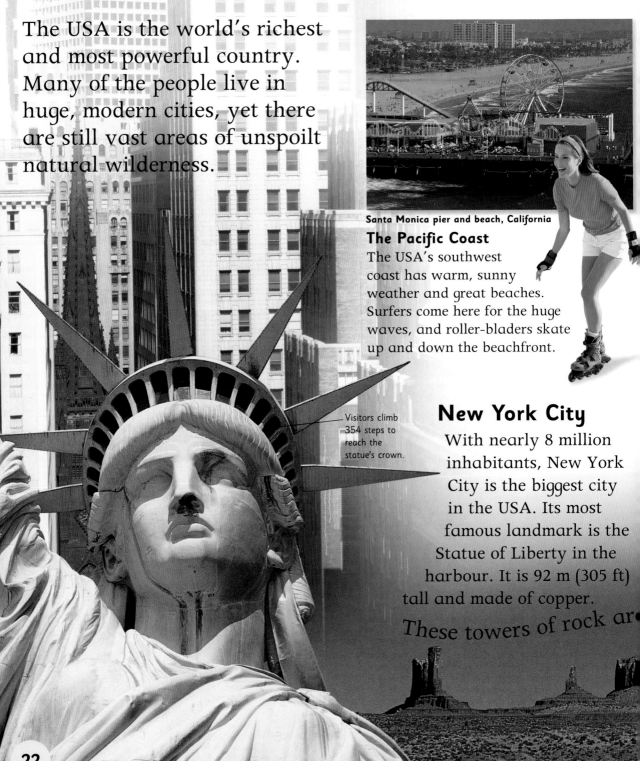

Santa Monica pier and beach, California

The Pacific Coast

The USA's southwest coast has warm, sunny weather and great beaches. Surfers come here for the huge waves, and roller-bladers skate up and down the beachfront.

Visitors climb 354 steps to reach the statue's crown.

New York City

With nearly 8 million inhabitants, New York City is the biggest city in the USA. Its most famous landmark is the Statue of Liberty in the harbour. It is 92 m (305 ft) tall and made of copper.

These towers of rock are

What is the hottest place in the USA?

Hawaii

The Hawaiian islands are the tops of volcanoes in the Pacific Ocean. Mount Kilauea has been erupting for years. Its lava flows into the sea and makes huge clouds of steam.

The Mississippi River

The Mississippi is North America's longest river. Barges carry cargos like oil, coal, and steel along it. Here the Mississippi is flowing past the Gateway Arch in St Louis, Missouri.

American alligator

Deserts and canyons

Southwestern USA is hot and dry. There are spectacular rocky towers called mesas, cactus-filled deserts, and deep canyons.

Swamps and alligators

There are huge grassy swamps called the Everglades in the state of Florida. The swamps are home to all sorts of wild animals, including alligators, panthers, and turtles.

...he crumbling remains of ancient mountains.

get going

Make an American flag like the one in the back of this book. Draw 7 red stripes on a sheet of paper, but leave a corner blank. Colour the corner blue and stick 50 small small white stars on it.

The Capitol building, Washington, DC.

Life in the USA

The USA is one of the world's most diverse countries. Most Americans are descended from people who moved here from other countries.

Capitol in the capital

Washington, DC, is the capital of the USA and home of the US government. Senators and congressmen meet in the Capitol building to make laws.

The city of New Orleans is the home of jazz.

Musical roots

Modern rock and pop music grew from jazz and blues, which were invented by African Americans about 100 years ago.

Independence Day

The USA became an independent country on 4 July 1776. The Fourth of July is a holiday called Independence Day. There are parties and big parades through the streets.

Independence Day parade

Where is Hollywood?

American food

America's food is as varied as its people.

Hamburgers are not made from ham, but from ground beef.

Clam chowder is seafood soup from New England, northeast USA.

Tex-Mex is a mixture of flavours from Texas and Mexico.

Gumbo is a spicy soup from Louisiana, made with meat and seafood.

American Indians

American Indians have lived in the USA for thousands of years. Today, about one in 100 Americans is American Indian.

These girls are wearing the traditional clothes of Navajo Indians. The Navajo live in Arizona and New Mexico.

American football

American football

The top spectator sport in the USA is American football. More than 40 million people a year go to watch games, often in big stadiums.

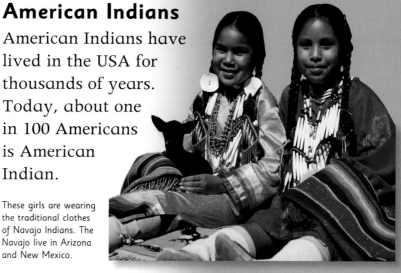

Rodeo rider on a bull

The Oscar award is given for excellence in making films.

© A.M.P.A.S.®

Rodeo rider

People visit rodeos to watch cowboys show off their riding skills. The cowboy tries to stay on a bucking horse or bull as long as he can.

Film industry

American films are watched all over the world. Hollywood is the home of the film industry.

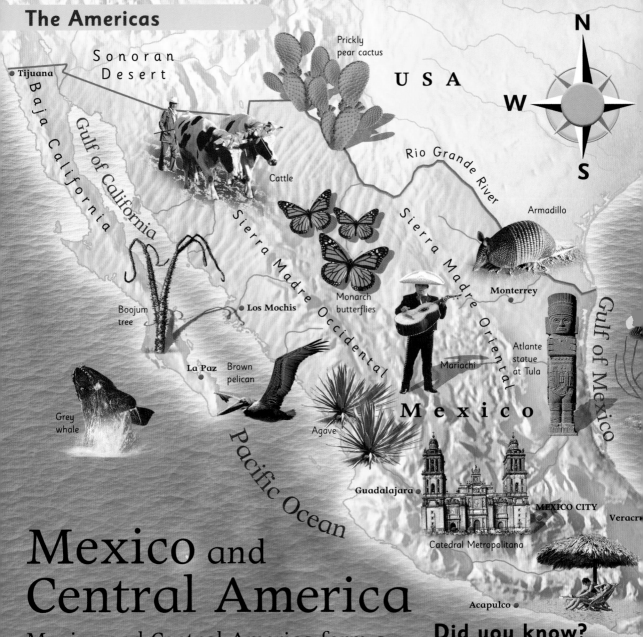

Prickly pear cactus

Sonoran Desert

Tijuana

U S A

N

W E

S

Baja California

Gulf of California

Rio Grande River

Armadillo

Cattle

Sierra Madre Occidental

Sierra Madre Oriental

Monterrey

Boojum tree

Los Mochis

Monarch butterflies

Atlante statue at Tula

Gulf of Mexico

Grey whale

La Paz

Brown pelican

Agave

Mariachi

M e x i c o

Pacific Ocean

Guadalajara

MEXICO CITY

Veracruz

Catedral Metropolitana

Acapulco

Mexico and Central America

Mexico and Central America form a natural bridge linking the USA to South America. The north of Mexico is dry and dusty. As you travel south, the weather gets rainier and the land becomes greener, with lush rainforests covering mountains and volcanoes.

Did you know?

Coffee beans and bananas are Costa Rica's most important crops.

Chocolate was first made in Mexico, from the seeds of the cacao tree.

Sugar cane from Central America and the Caribbean is used to make sugar.

26

How do spider monkeys use their tails?

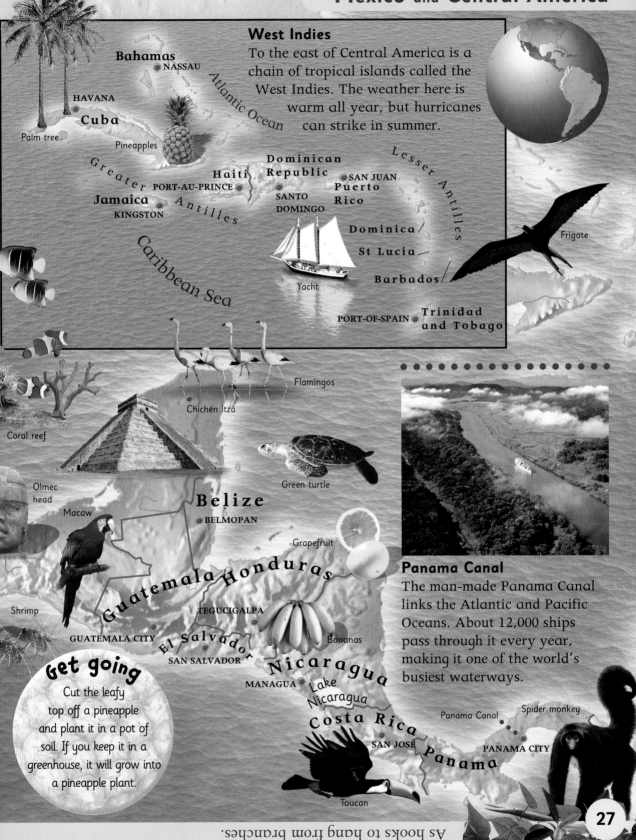

West Indies

To the east of Central America is a chain of tropical islands called the West Indies. The weather here is warm all year, but hurricanes can strike in summer.

Bahamas
NASSAU

Atlantic Ocean

HAVANA
Cuba

Palm tree

Pineapples

Greater Antilles

Haiti
PORT-AU-PRINCE

Dominican Republic
SANTO DOMINGO

SAN JUAN
Puerto Rico

Lesser Antilles

Jamaica
KINGSTON

Dominica

St Lucia

Frigate

Caribbean Sea

Yacht

Barbados

PORT-OF-SPAIN
Trinidad and Tobago

Flamingos

Coral reef

Chichén Itzá

Olmec head

Macaw

Green turtle

Belize
BELMOPAN

Grapefruit

Shrimp

Guatemala **Honduras**

TEGUCIGALPA

Bananas

GUATEMALA CITY

El Salvador
SAN SALVADOR

Nicaragua
MANAGUA
Lake Nicaragua

Panama Canal

The man-made Panama Canal links the Atlantic and Pacific Oceans. About 12,000 ships pass through it every year, making it one of the world's busiest waterways.

Panama Canal

Spider monkey

Costa Rica
SAN JOSÉ

Panama
PANAMA CITY

Get going

Cut the leafy top off a pineapple and plant it in a pot of soil. If you keep it in a greenhouse, it will grow into a pineapple plant.

Toucan

As hooks to hang from branches.

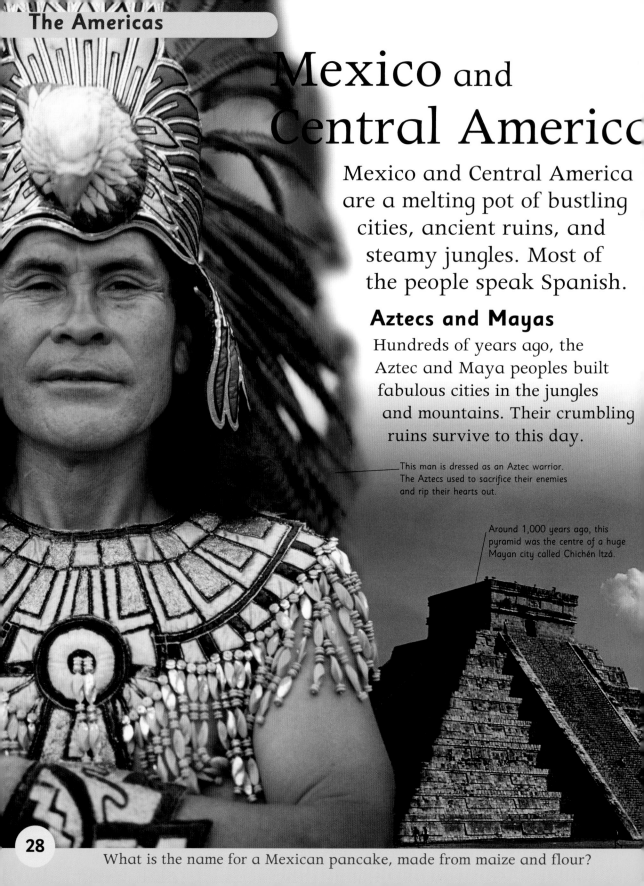

Mexico and Central America

Mexico and Central America are a melting pot of bustling cities, ancient ruins, and steamy jungles. Most of the people speak Spanish.

Aztecs and Mayas

Hundreds of years ago, the Aztec and Maya peoples built fabulous cities in the jungles and mountains. Their crumbling ruins survive to this day.

This man is dressed as an Aztec warrior. The Aztecs used to sacrifice their enemies and rip their hearts out.

Around 1,000 years ago, this pyramid was the centre of a huge Mayan city called Chichén Itzá.

What is the name for a Mexican pancake, made from maize and flour?

Agriculture

Central America is warm and wet – perfect weather for tropical crops like bananas, maize, avocados, and peppers. Farmers sell their crops in the busy local markets.

Mexico City

Mexico's capital was built on the ruins of an ancient Aztec city. It is now one of the world's biggest cities, with 20 million people.

Tacos and tortillas

Mexicans like spicy food flavoured with chillis. These are tacos – fried pancakes full of meat and vegetables. The pancakes are called tortillas.

Caribbean paradise

The sunny islands of the Caribbean attract tourists by the million. They come to laze on beautiful, sandy beaches, swim in the warm sea, and snorkel over coral reefs.

Get going

Get a slice of bread and roll it out flat using a rolling pin. Now add your favourite filling and roll the bread around it. You've just made a Mexican enchilada!

A tortilla (pronounced "tor-teeya").

South America

A vast chain of mountains runs the length of this continent. On its western side is the world's driest desert. On the east is the biggest rainforest.

Equator walkabout

The Equator is an imaginary line around Earth's middle. It would take you a month to walk across just the South American part of it!

Venezuela

CARACAS

Orinoco

Agrias butterfly

Cartagena

BOGOTÁ

Colombia

QUITO

Ecuador

Guyana

GEORGETOWN

PARAMARIBO

Suriname

CAYENNE

French Guiana

Angel Falls

Equator

Amazon Rainforest

Manaus

River Amazon

Belém

Capybara

Brazil nuts

Bananas

Brazil

Jaguar

Condor

Machu Picchu

Peru

LIMA

Andes Mountains

Lake Titicaca

Arequipa

Bolivia

LA PAZ

Pacific Ocean

What is the highest mountain in the Andes?

Oil rig

football

Rio de Janeiro

São Paulo

Sugar Loaf Mountain

Atlantic Ocean

Green turtle

Gaucho

Paraguay

ASUNCIÓN

Llama

Argentina

Pampas grass

Uruguay

MONTEVIDEO

BUENOS AIRES

Pampas

Bahia Blanca

Chile

Atacama Desert

Andes Mountains

Aconcagua

Valparaíso

SANTIAGO

Sheep farming

Patagonia

Magellan penguins

Mackerel

Cape Horn

The southern tip of South America is called Cape Horn. The seas around it are so stormy that hundreds of ships have been shipwrecked there.

Cape Horn

Can you find...

The world's highest capital?
La Paz, Bolivia, is 3,632 m (11,916 ft) above sea level.

The world's highest waterfall?
Angel Falls in Venezuela measures 979 m (3,212 ft) from top to bottom.

The world's driest town?
Arica in Chile's Atacama Desert has an annual rainfall of zero!

Aconcagua, which is 6,960 m (22,834 ft) high.

South America

One third of South America is covered by a huge jungle called the Amazon rainforest. To the east and south of the rainforest are rich grasslands, enormous cattle ranches, and South America's biggest cities.

Scarlet macaw

Forest life

Native people have lived in the Amazon jungle for thousands of years. They survive by hunting and gathering wild food, without harming the forest.

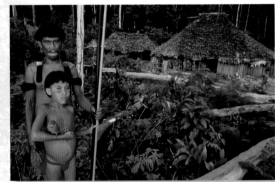

Yanomami village in the Amazon rainforest.

Deadly animals

The Amazon rainforest is home to all sorts of dangerous creatures.

Forest people use **poison-dart frogs** to make deadly poison for arrows.

The **jaguar** is a very secretive cat. It is a good swimmer and climber.

Piranhas are vicious fish with very sharp teeth. They hunt in packs.

The **boa constrictor** kills animals by squeezing them to death.

Gauchos

Argentinian gauchos are like American cowboys. They work on vast ranches in the pampas grasslands of Argentina, where they look after cattle and horses.

Dug-out canoe on the Amazon

What language do most Brazilians speak?

Highest waterfall
Angel Falls in Venezuela is the world's highest waterfall. The water tumbles off a flat-topped mountain and plunges 980 m (3,215 ft) to the ground. That's three times the height of New York's Empire State Building.

Granadillas grow on jungle vines.

Forest fruits
The granadilla (a kind of passion fruit) is one of many exotic fruits that grow in tropical parts of South America.

Rio de Janeiro
A statue of Christ towers over Rio de Janeiro, Brazil's second-largest city. In the bay is the dome-shaped Sugar Loaf Mountain.

Carnival
Every year, Rio de Janeiro holds a spectacular carnival that lasts four days. People dress up in brilliant costumes and dance through the streets, blowing whistles and singing.

Portuguese.

Life in the Andes

The Andes stretch all the way down South America, forming the world's longest mountain range. The people and animals that live in the Andes are used to the cold, thin air.

Condor
The Andean condor is a huge bird of prey. In flight, its wings measure 3 m (10 ft) from tip to tip.

Machu Picchu

High in the Andes in Peru are the ruins of an ancient city called Machu Picchu. The city was built about 500 years ago by people called Incas.

Llamas
A llama is like a tall sheep. People in the Andes keep llamas for their warm wool, their milk and meat, and for carrying cargo.

What is the most southerly city in the world?

Atacama Desert

The Atacama is the largest desert in South America. It is officially the driest place on Earth because it hardly ever rains here.

Valparaíso

Sandwiched between the mountains and the coast is Valparaíso, one of Chile's biggest cities. It is Chile's main port.

Get going

Make some panpipes. Join a row of ten straws with sticky tape. Cut the bottoms of the straws at an angle. Blow across the straws to play the pipes.

Mountain people

Many people who live in the Andes are South American Indians. Their families have lived in the Andes for hundreds of years.

People from the Andean city of Cuzco, Peru, wear very colourful clothes.

Pan pipes

The pan pipes are a traditional Andean musical instrument. They are made from hollow reeds or bamboo.

Sailing on top of the world

At 3,800 metres (12,450 ft) high, Lake Titicaca is the highest lake in the world that ships can sail on. Local people fish the lake in boats made from reeds.

Africa

Africa is a vast, sun-baked continent, famous for its amazing wildlife. In the north and south are hot deserts. Between the deserts are swampy rainforests and grasslands full of wild animals.

Asia

Horn of Africa

Djibouti

ADDIS ABABA

Ethiopia

Great Rift Valley

Eritrea

ASMARA

Red Sea

KHARTOUM

Southern Sudan

Nubian Desert

Nile felucca boat

Sudan

Aswan

River Nile

Suez Canal

CAIRO

Pyramids

Egypt

Cheetah

Mediterranean Sea

Gulf of Sirte

TRIPOLI

Al 'Aziziyah

Libya

Bedouin weaver

Chad

Lake Chad

NDJAMENA

Hippopotamus

Central African Rep.

Cameroon

Lion

TUNIS

Tunisia

ALGIERS

Erg Tifernine

Ahaggar Mountains

Sahara Desert

Niger

Ostriches

Sahel

NIAMEY

Nigeria

ABUJA

Ait Benhaddou mud fortress, Morocco

Atlas Mountains

RABAT

Morocco

Western Sahara

LAAYOUNE

Algeria

Tuareg nomads

Mali

River Niger

Burkina

BAMAKO

Bambara village

Benin

Togo

Ghana

Ivory Coast

Liberia

Peanuts

Mauritania

NOUAKCHOTT

Senegal

DAKAR

Gambia

Guinea-Bissau

Guinea

Sierra Leone

Atlantic Ocean

N E S W

How long is Africa from north to south?

Can you find...

The highest point in Africa?
Mount Kilimanjaro in Tanzania is 5,895 m (19,341 ft) tall.

One of the world's highest sand dunes? Erg Tifernine in the Sahara is 400 m (1,300 ft) tall.

The hottest place on Earth?
Al 'Aziziyah, in Libya, has had temperatures of 58°C (136.4°F).

The Suez Canal
This canal is a man-made waterway that runs from the Red Sea to the Mediterranean. It provides a short cut for ships travelling from Europe to Asia.

Savanna wildlife
Much of Africa is covered by a type of grassland called savanna. Huge herds of grazing animals live on the savanna, as well as lions, hyenas, and cheetahs.

Atlantic Ocean

About 8,000 km (5,000 miles).

Gabon
Congo
River Congo
Lowland gorilla
KINSHASA
Dem. Rep. of Congo
LUANDA
Oil rig
Hornbill
Angola
Zambia
LUSAKA
Zebra
Zambezi River
Namibia
WINDHOEK
Giraffe
Namib Desert
Victoria Falls
Botswana
Kalahari Desert
Tin and copper mining
Springbok
Zimbabwe
South Africa
Cape Town
Cape of Good Hope
PRETORIA
MAPUTO
Swaziland
Lesotho
Ndeble house
Rwanda
Burundi
KAMPALA
Lake Victoria
Kenya
NAIROBI
Mount Kilimanjaro
Tanzania
DODOMA
Serengeti
Masai herder
Elephant
Malawi
Great Rift Valley
Mozambique
Mozambique Channel
Madagascar
ANTANANARIVO
Lemur
Chameleon
Dhow sailing boat

Madagascar
The island of Madagascar is home to tree-dwelling animals called lemurs. They have faces like cats but bodies like monkeys.

Life in Africa

There are about 50 countries in Africa, but hundreds of different peoples and more than 1,000 languages. Most African people are farmers who live in the countryside. In recent times, many people have moved into cities.

Villagers in Ghana carrying water

Health and disease

Poor health is a problem in some parts of Africa. Many Africans have to walk for hours every day to fetch clean water. Diseases such as malaria are common.

Mosquitoes spread malaria when they bite people.

Masai people often wear lots of red to scare off lions.

Masai necklaces

The Masai people of east Africa lead a traditional way of life, herding their cows across the land. Masai women wear colourful beaded necklaces to show off how rich they are.

What is the world's largest continent?

Living in the city

One out of every five Africans lives in bustling cities, such as Cape Town. People move to the cities to find work and a better life.

Drummers from Ghana

African music

Africa people love music and dancing. These musicians come from Ghana in west Africa. Their drums are made from animal skins pulled tight by strings.

Safaris save animals

Tourists come to Africa's savanna (grassland) to see the wildlife. The money the tourists spend helps to save rare animals, such as rhinos.

Rainforest life

In the rainforests of central Africa, some people get their food from the wild. They travel through the forest, hunting animals and gathering fruit.

Animals roam the savanna in huge herds.

African deserts

The biggest desert in the world, the Sahara, stretches right across northern Africa. Two more deserts, the Namib and the Kalahari, are located in southern Africa.

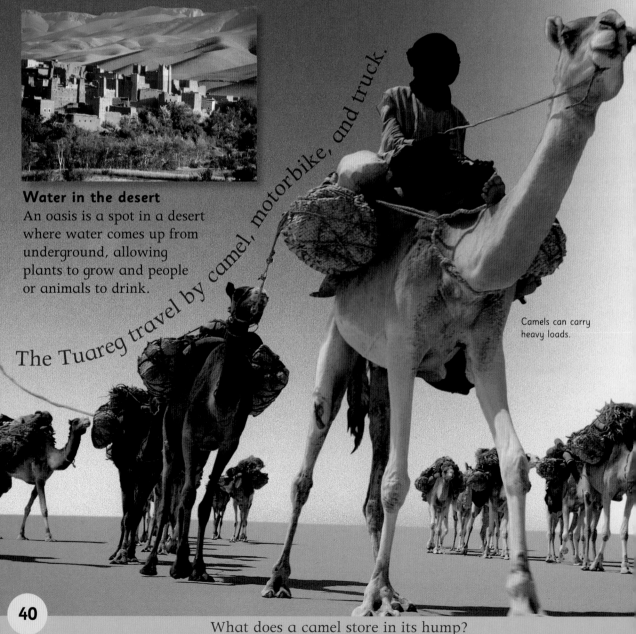

Water in the desert
An oasis is a spot in a desert where water comes up from underground, allowing plants to grow and people or animals to drink.

The Tuareg travel by camel, motorbike, and truck.

Trading in the desert
The Tuareg people are traders who live in the Sahara Desert. The men cover their faces with long blue scarves.

Camels can carry heavy loads.

What does a camel store in its hump?

Saharan wildlife

The Sahara is baking hot by day and freezing cold at night. Even so, lots of animals live there.

The **fennec fox** has huge ears that let heat escape from its body.

Horned vipers lie hidden in sand, looking for animals to eat.

The **jerboa** gets all the water it needs from the seeds it eats.

Desert locusts form huge swarms that can destroy crops.

A **scorpion** has a sting at the end of its tail for killing the animals it eats.

Desert nomads

Desert nomads spend their lives on the move. They travel from oasis to oasis by camel and live in tents.

The San

The San are people from the Kalahari Desert. Today many San live in villages and towns, but some still lead a traditional way of life, moving around the desert hunting for food.

The San use hollow ostrich eggs as flasks to carry water in the desert.

Get going

Make a nomad's tent. Throw a large sheet over a table so that it hangs down to the floor. Cover the floor under the table with colourful rugs and comfy cushions.

San hunters with poisoned arrows

Dogon dancers

The Dogon people live in Mali on the edge of the Sahara Desert. These Dogon are imitating long-legged birds in a traditional stilt dance.

The River Nile

Life in northeast Africa would be impossible without the Nile, the world's longest river. It flows right across the Sahara Desert, providing vital water and a highway for boats.

Lake Victoria is the main source of the Nile.

The route of the Nile
The Nile begins in Uganda and flows 6,700 km (4,200 miles) north, passing through Sudan and Egypt.

Aswan dams
At Aswan in Egypt, two huge dams have been built to store water and to generate electricity.

Sailing the Nile

In Egypt, people sail up and down the Nile on wooden boats called feluccas. It hardly ever rains in Egypt, so the crew sleep on the open deck at night.

Abu Simbel
The Abu Simbel temples were built by the ancient Egyptians. Engineers moved them to save them from being drowned when the Aswan High Dam was built.

Who was buried in Egypt's biggest pyramid?

City on the Nile
Cairo is the capital of Egypt and the biggest city in Africa. Around 10 million people live in Cairo, many of them in crowded slums.

Nile Delta from space

Nile Delta
The Nile dumps lots of silt at its mouth, forming a muddy area called a delta. Crops grow especially well here.

Nile crops
These crops grow on the banks of the Nile.

Wheat is grown for making flour, which is used in bread-making.

Dates are delicious fruits. Date tree leaves are woven into baskets.

Fibres from **cotton seeds** are used to make yarn and fabrics.

The Pyramids
Huge pyramids stand in the desert near Cairo. The pyramids were built thousands of years ago as tombs for ancient kings called pharaohs.

The Sphinx has a lion's body and a man's head.

Egyptian farmers use donkeys to pull carts.

Farming on the Nile
Farmers take water from the Nile to irrigate their fields. There is a narrow strip of farmland on each bank of the river. The Sahara Desert lies beyond the fields.

Pharaoh Khufu (Cheops).

Scandinavia

The northernmost part of Europe is Scandinavia – a region of dense pine forests, snowy mountains, and craggy coastlines.

Iceland

Iceland is a volcanic island in the far north Atlantic Ocean. It has hundreds of hot springs and geysers.

Greenland Sea

Church of Hallingrimur

Vatnajokull (ice sheet)

Geyser

REYKJAVIK

Arctic Ocean

North Cape

Fishing trawler

Tromso

Puffin

Vestfjorden

Russian Federation

Sami man with reindeer

Wolf

Sauna

Paper mill

Oulu

River Kemijoki

Gulf of Bothnia

Lapland

Mining

Lynx

Grey seal

Sweden

Kjolen Mountains

Wolverine

Norwegian Sea

Atlantic Ocean

44

Which Scandinavian warriors raided Europe in 800–1050 AD?

Finland

Rainbow trout

Cathedral,
Helsinki

Gulf of Finland

HELSINKI

Åland
Islands

STOCKHOLM

The Øresund Bridge

The Øresund Bridge links Copenhagen in Denmark to Malmö in Sweden. There are three parts to the bridge – an underground tunnel, an artificial island, and a bridge over the sea. Together, they are 16 km (10 miles) long.

Golden eagle

Cross-country
skiing

City Hall,
Stockholm

Rune stone

Gotland

Öland

Baltic Sea

Swedish
glass

Bornholm

N

W — E

S

Stave church

Mount Galdhøppigen
2,469 m (8,100 ft)

N o r w a y

Lake
Vänern

Lake
Vättern

Gothenburg

COPENHAGEN

Malmö

Little Mermaid statue,
Copenhagen

Nord Fjord

Sogne Fjord

Bergen

Hardanger Fjord

Bokn Fjord

Stavanger

OSLO

Oslo Fjord

Sculptures in
Vigeland Park, Oslo

Dairy
farming

D e n m a r k

Pig farming

Lego

Faeroe Islands

These islands are part of Denmark. They lie halfway between Iceland and Scotland.

Tórshavn

Herring

North Sea

The Vikings.

Scandinavia

Scandinavians enjoy a spectacular landscape and a high standard of living. But they also have to cope with long, dark, icy winters.

Ski jumper, Norway

Pine forests cover much of Scandinavia.

Winter sports
Winter sports are very popular in Scandinavia. Many top ski jumpers come from this region.

All the houses in Legoland are built from Lego.

Legoland
The Legoland theme park in Denmark is built from 50 million Lego™ bricks. Lego was invented in Denmark in 1949.

Viking ships
The Vikings lived in Scandinavia 1,000 years ago. They raided other countries in longships like this one.

Timber industry
In Scandinavia, millions of trees are grown for their wood. The timber is made into houses, furniture, and paper.

What is a Finnish steam room called?

Wildlife

The animals that live in Scandinavia are well adapted to the cold.

Arctic foxes have thick white fur for warmth and camouflage in the snow.

The **lynx** is a type of cat from the forests of Norway and Sweden.

Puffins are small seabirds. They swim underwater to catch fish.

Elks are large deer. Their huge antlers can be 2 metres (6.5 ft) wide.

Naturally hot
Iceland has many volcanoes, geysers, and hot springs. The water in this lake is heated by hot rocks deep underground.

Norwegian fjords

Hundreds of narrow valleys cut into the coast of Norway. They are called fjords. Ships can shelter here from bad weather.

Lapland

The north of Scandinavia is called Lapland. The people who live there are Lapps or Sami. Some Lapps herd reindeer for their fur, meat, and milk.

UK and Ireland

The United Kingdom is made up of England, Scotland, Wales, and Northern Ireland. Ireland is a separate country. Most of the people in the UK and Ireland speak English as their main language.

The Royal Family

England and Scotland had separate royal families until 1603, when they joined together to form the United Kingdom. Queen Elizabeth II is the current Head of State.

Shetland Islands

Orkney Islands

Thurso

Outer Hebrides

Red deer

Skye

Highland cow

Mull

Loch Ness Monster

Aberdeen

Grampian Mountains

Ben Nevis 1,343 m (4,406 ft)

Scotland

River Forth

Glasgow

Bagpiper

Edinburgh

Edinburgh Castle

Giant's Causeway

Northern

North Sea

Angel of the North

What is the name of the Queen's official residence in London?

North Sea oil rig

Yacht

Norfolk Broads

Cambridge

Dover

Eurotunnel to France

Middlesbrough

Kingston upon Hull

Big Ben

LONDON

Brighton

Royal Pavillion

England

Pennines

District

Blackpool Tower

Manchester

Football

Birmingham

Crufts dog show

Oxford

River Thames

River Severn

Isle of Wight

Stonehenge

English Channel

France

Liverpool

Snowdonia

Cambrian Mountains

Cardiff

Wales

Portland Bill lighthouse

Isle of Man

Douglas

Irish Sea

Sheep

Exmoor

Exeter

Dartmoor

Eden Project

Guinness

DUBLIN

Surfing

Land's End

Isles of Scilly

The Eden Project, Cornwall

These giant greenhouses are home to lots of plants from different areas of the world. People can visit here to learn how important nature is to the future of the planet.

Ireland

Galway

Blarney Castle

Cork

Jaunting car

N E S W

UK and Ireland

The islands that make up the UK and Ireland are called the British Isles. The British Isles are famous for their history, traditions, and for their green – though rainy – countryside.

The London Eye

London is the capital of the UK and the site of the London Eye – a gigantic ferris wheel that gives tourists a stunning view over the city.

Passengers ride the Eye in glass capsules.

Fish and chips

British food has been influenced by many cultures, but the traditional meal of fried fish and chips is still a popular dish

Stately home

Windsor Castle near London is one of the Queen's homes. It is the largest occupied castle in the world and has around 1,000 rooms. Certain parts of the castle are open to tourists.

Grenadier guards wear a tall hat made from the fur of Canadian black bears.

The Queen's private army of guards are called beefeaters.

Which Welsh village has the longest place name in Europe?

Down the pub

Nearly every town and village in the UK and Ireland boasts at least one pub, where people go to relax and meet their friends. Irish pubs serve a famous type of beer called Guinness, which is jet black and very frothy.

A pint of Guinness

British sports

Sports invented in Britain are now played all over the world.

Cricket is played in summer. Some matches last for five days.

Football is the world's most popular sport, watched by billions.

Rugby is played with an oval ball that the players pick up and run with.

Scottish lakes are called lochs.

Rocky coast

Rugged cliffs and strange rock formations dot the north coast of Northern Ireland. The wobbly Carrick-a-rede Rope Bridge leads to a tiny island.

Highland cow

Scottish highlands

Northern Scotland has some of the UK's quietest countryside, with miles of rolling mountains and glassy lakes. There are few people here, apart from farmers and hikers.

Football and rugby

Football and rugby matches attract huge crowds of fans in the UK. English and Scottish people are great football fans. Welsh people also like rugby.

The Low Countries

Belgium, the Netherlands, and Luxembourg are called the Low Countries because they are so flat. They are also sometimes called Benelux – the first letters of BElgium, NEtherlands and LUXembourg.

Netherlands

Germany

Avocet

Cattle

Cyclist

Ice skating

Horses

River Rhine

Arnhem

West Frisian Islands

Waddenzee

Flevoland

Windmills

Clogs

IJsselmeer

Tern

Cheese porters

AMSTERDAM

Tulips

Barge

Rotterdam

Antwerp Cathedral

North Sea

The Hague

Cubic Houses

Fishing

Herring

Dams to stop floods from sea

Bruges Town Hall

Bruges

Ostend

N E S W

What is another name for the Netherlands?

Did you know..?

Brussels is the capital of Europe. It is the centre of the European Union and home of the European Parliament.

900 windmills along the Netherlands' coast help to keep the land drained.

Wooden clogs were first invented by Dutch workmen 600 years ago.

The Atomium

Belgium

BRUSSELS

Chocolates

Lace making

Crystal   Liège

Charleroi

River Meuse

Deer

Ardennes

Ardennes Forest

Wild boar

Beer

France

Vianden castle

Luxembourg

LUXEMBOURG

Amsterdam

The tall houses lining the canals of Amsterdam were built by rich spice merchants hundreds of years ago. Each one is unique, and many are crooked because they are built on marshy land.

The Low Countries

Large parts of the Low Countries used to be underwater, but people worked out how to turn the shallow sea into farmland. The area is now famous for growing flowers.

Amsterdam

People sometimes call Amsterdam "the Venice of the north" because the city is riddled with canals and full of beautiful old houses. Cycling is popular here as there are few cars in the town centre and no hills.

The Dutch make 3 million pairs of clogs (wooden shoes) each year. Farmers used to wear shoes like this for working in boggy fields.

Get going

Make a windmill. Cut a cross from paper 10 cm across. Twist each arm slightly the same way. Pin the centre to a pencil and blow on the back to make it spin.

Cheese market

On Fridays, Dutch cheese-makers hold a traditional market in the town of Alkmaar to sell huge wheels of cheese. The most popular cheeses are Edam, which is covered with red wax, and Gouda.

How much of the Netherlands used to be under the sea?

The medieval castle at Vianden, Luxembourg

Dutch master
Vincent van Gogh (1853–90) was a brilliant, but mad, Dutch artist who cut off his own ear. He painted this self-portrait in 1889.

Luxembourg
Luxembourg is a tiny, but rich, country with beautiful scenery and spectacular castles. The people speak a language called Letzebuergesch.

Windmills
The Dutch once used windmills to pump water out of low land, but now they mostly use electric pumps. Dykes (earth banks) stop the water flooding back in.

The Atomium
This strange building in Brussels is a model of nine iron atoms, enlarged 165 billion times. Visitors can go inside six of the "atoms", which are joined by escalators.

About one third.

France

France is the biggest country in western Europe. Its capital is the city of Paris, site of the Eiffel Tower. France is famous for its scenic countryside, which is dotted with sleepy villages and fairytale castles called châteaux.

English Channel

Breton woman

Mont St-Michel

Bayeux Tapes

Le M race

Rennes

Le Ma

Standing Stones (Carnac)

Mackerel

Beef cattle

Atlantic Ocean

Mont St-Michel

A towering abbey sits on the island of Mont St-Michel off the north coast of France. At low tide, people can walk across the sand to get to Mont St-Michel.

Brar

Bordeaux

Bay of Biscay

Wine

Cave Paint at Lasca

Biarritz

Aeroplane manufacturing

Tou

Pyrenees Mountains

Where in France would you find pink flamingos and wild horses?

Calais

Belgium

Lille

The Channel
Tunnel

Pollock

River Seine

Eiffel Tower

PARIS

France

World War I Memorial
(Vimy)

Germany

Champagne

Boules

River Loire

Nancy

Château de
Chambord

Chapel of
Notre Dame
Du Haut

Strasbourg

Vosges Mountains

Mustard

Dijon

Cycling

Jura Mountains

Garlic

Massif Central

Lyon

Edible
snails

Mont Blanc
4,807 m
(15,771 ft)

quefort
heese

River Rhône

Alps

ennes Mountains

Sunflowers

Skiing

Montpellier

Camargue

Casinos

Tourism

Marseille

Nice

Toulon

Cannes

Monaco

Camargue horses

Corsica

This French island is in
the Mediterranean Sea
next to Italy (see page 68).
It has a beautiful rocky
coast with lots of beaches.

Napoleon

Bastia

Ajaccio

Tourism

The marshes of the Camargue.

France

Perfumes, bread, edible snails, and champagne are a few of the things that France is famous for. Millions of tourists visit Paris each year to see its beautiful buildings, parks and museums.

Café culture

French people love to sit in cafés and watch the world go by. This café is on a wide avenue called the Champs-Élysées.

A famous landmark

The Eiffel Tower is the most famous landmark in France. It is 300 metres (984 feet) high and was built in 1889. Tourists can go up to the top platform.

Visitors can walk up to the first and second floors.

get going

Fields of sunflowers are a common sight in France. Grow your own sunflower by planting a seed in a pot of soil in spring. Water it every week and it will be taller than you by summer.

How many people visit the Eiffel Tower each year?

Food and wine

French restaurants serve some of the best food in the world. France is also famous for making wine.

Snails are a French delicacy. They are cooked in their shells with garlic.

Croissants are made from fluffy pastry. People eat them for breakfast.

Champagne is a fizzy white wine. It is made in an area called Champagne.

Luxury houses

A large French country house is called a château. This one is Château d'Azay-le-Rideau. It was built 500 years ago and is surrounded by a lake.

Fast trains

The French TGV is the fastest express train in the world. It speeds along its special track at 300 km (190 miles) per hour.

Cheese making

France makes 400 kinds of cheese, many of which are eaten all over the world. This cheese-maker taps the cheese to check if it has any holes.

About 200 cyclists enter the race.

Cyclists on the Tour de France, a three-week race.

Cycle racing

The Tour de France is the world's greatest cycle race and lasts for thousands of miles. French people stop work or school to watch the cyclists as they ride through town.

Many French farmers grow grapes for making wine.

About 6 million.

Germany and the Alps

The north of Germany is low and flat, but the land gradually rises towards the south. Switzerland and Austria lie in the heart of the Alps – Europe's tallest and most spectacular mountains.

Berlin Wall
A long wall used to divide the city of Berlin into communist and western halves. In 1989 the people of Berlin tore the wall down and reunited the city.

N
E
W
S

Poland

River Oder

Rügen

Stork

BERLIN

Chemical industry

Zwinger Palace

Brandenburg Gate

Leipzig

Halle

Lake Müritz

Volkswagen cars

River Elbe

Fehmarn

Heidschnuke sheep

Kiel Canal

Kiel

River Elbe

Hamburg

Hanover

Wheat

Bremen

Germany

Beef cattle

North Sea

Container ship

Cologne Cathedral

River Rhine

Düsseldorf

Which composer was born in Salzburg, Austria, in 1756?

Czech Republic

Thuringian Forest

Bohemian Forest

Austria

Spanish riding school

Neusiedler Lake

VIENNA

River Danube

Mountain climbing

Linz

Graz

Mozart

Snow boarding

Salzburg

Austrian Alps

Oktoberfest

Chamois goat

Lake Chiemsee

Munich

Bavarian Alps

Innsbruck

Marmot

Zugspitze 2,962 m (9,718 ft)

Nuremberg

River Main

River Danube

Swabian Alps

Ulm

Cheese

Neuschwanstein Castle

Lake Constance

VADUZ

Davos

Liechtenstein

Frankfurt skyline

Frankfurt

Mannheim

Heidelberg

Wine

Mercedes

Stuttgart

Black Forest

Freiburg

River Rhine

Zurich

Swiss army knife

BERN

Switzerland

Swiss Alps

Alpine horn

Chocolate

River Rhône

Matterhorn 4,478 m (14,692 ft)

Geneva

France

Germany and the Alps

Germany, Austria, and Switzerland are rich industrial countries. They make and export many high-quality goods, including cars, watches, and chocolates.

Pyramid peak

The Matterhorn in Switzerland is one of the tallest mountains in the Alps. Some people have fallen to their death trying to climb it.

Ice has carved the peak of the Matterhorn into a pyramid shape.

German industry

Volkswagens are made in Europe's biggest car factory, near Hanover in Germany. Car-making is one of Germany's main industries.

Winter sports

Millions of people come to the Alps every winter to ski and snowboard. Hikers and mountaineers walk in the valleys and scale the peaks.

How did farmers used to communicate in the Alps?

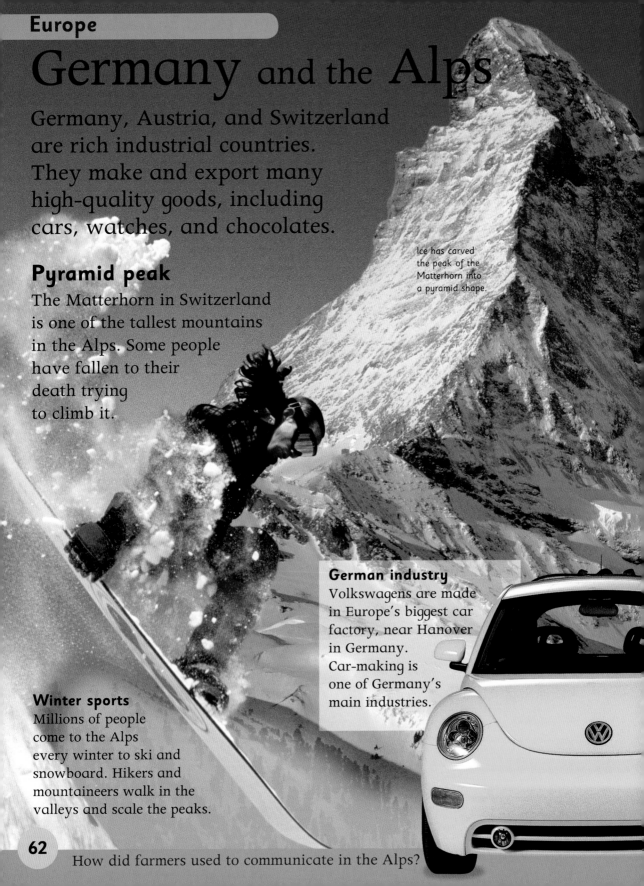

Alpine wildlife

Many plants and animals survive high in the Alps.

Edelweiss is a small flower that grows in Alpine meadows.

The **Alpine marmot** sleeps through the winter in its burrow.

The **chamois** grows a thick, woolly coat to keep it warm.

Neuschwanstein in Bavaria was the inspiration for Sleeping Beauty's castle in Disneyland.

German castles

Fabulous castles are scattered among the mountains of southern Germany. Neuschwanstein was built in 1869 by an eccentric king called Ludwig II.

Carnival time

Germans celebrate the end of winter with carnivals. In Cologne, people dress up in bright costumes and join the parades.

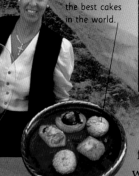

Viennese pastries are said to be the best cakes in the world.

Viennese coffee houses

Vienna in Austria is famous for its coffee houses, where people drink coffee and eat expensive cakes.

Alpine cows have bells so that farmers don't lose them on the mountainside.

Germany's waterways

Germany's cities are linked by a large network of canals and rivers. This cargo barge is on the River Neckar in the city of Heidelberg.

Swiss people eat more chocolate than anyone else in the world.

Dairy farming

Swiss farmers take their cows to high alpine meadows in summer. The cows' milk is used for making chocolates and cheese.

By yodelling (singing across mountain valleys).

Spain and Portugal

Spain and Portugal are in the sunny southwest corner of Europe. Together they make up a region called the Iberian Peninsula.

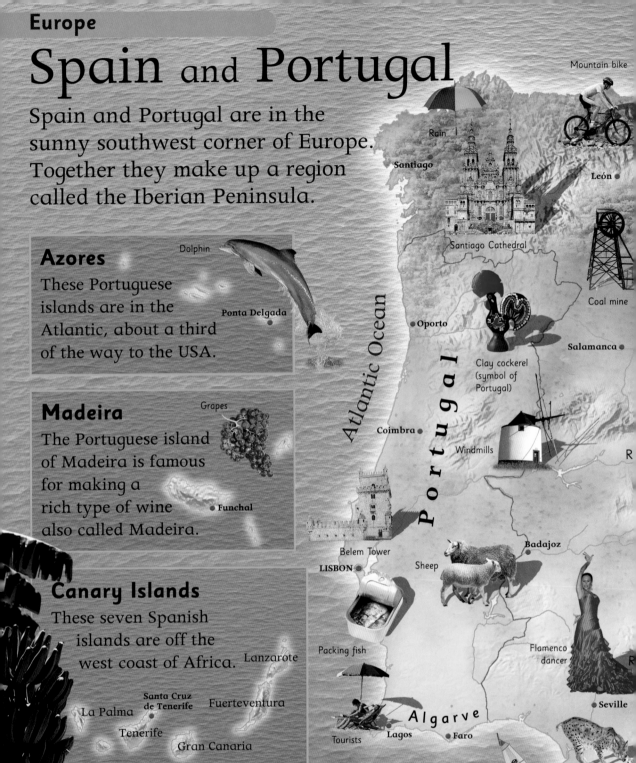

Mountain bike

Rain

Santiago

León

Santiago Cathedral

Coal mine

Azores

These Portuguese islands are in the Atlantic, about a third of the way to the USA.

Dolphin

Ponta Delgada

Atlantic Ocean

Oporto

Salamanca

Clay cockerel (symbol of Portugal)

Madeira

The Portuguese island of Madeira is famous for making a rich type of wine also called Madeira.

Grapes

Funchal

Coimbra

Windmills

P o r t u g a l

Belem Tower

LISBON

Sheep

Badajoz

Canary Islands

These seven Spanish islands are off the west coast of Africa.

Lanzarote

Santa Cruz de Tenerife

Fuerteventura

La Palma

Tenerife

Gran Canaria

Banana plantations

Packing fish

Flamenco dancer

Seville

Tourists

A l g a r v e

Lagos

Faro

Lynx

Crayfish

Wind surfing

Gibraltar

Which is the rainiest city in Spain?

France

Guggenheim
Museum
● Bilbao

Basque
Country

Mountain
goat

Pyrenees

Andorra

ANDORRA
LA VELLA

Skiing

N

Wild boar

Iberian Mountains

...adolid

Spain

Rioja wine

River Ebro

Barcelona

W   E

Roman aqueduct

Sagrada Familia
Cathedral, Barcelona

S

● MADRID

Sardines

Balearic Islands

Minorca

Mahón

Majorca

● Palma

Bull-fighting

Royal Palace

Paella

Albacete ●

● Valencia

Oranges

Ibiza

● Ibiza

Formentera

Mediterranean Sea

● Alicante

...alquivir

Andalusian horse

Costa Blanca

Guitar

...ndalusia

Olives
and oil

● Cartagena

Majorca
The Spanish
island of Majorca
is one of Europe's top
tourist destinations.
Its rugged coast has lots
of picturesque beaches.

● Granada

...ntains

● Malaga

Costa del Sol

Jet ski

Spain and Portugal

The streets of Spain and Portugal burst to life during their colourful festivals, or fiestas, but in the hot afternoons they can be sleepy and quiet.

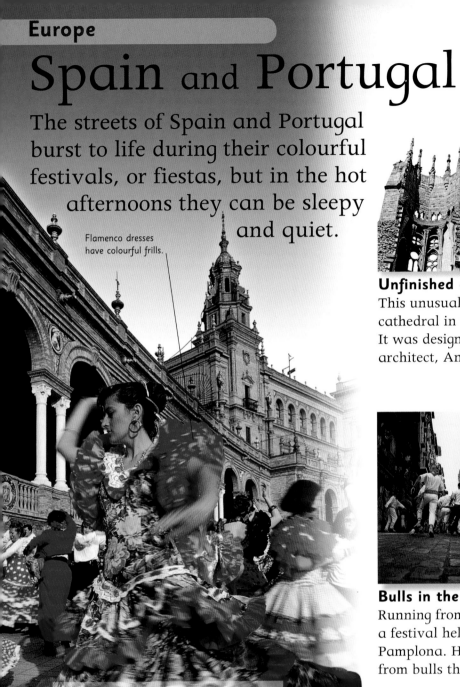

Flamenco dresses have colourful frills.

Unfinished cathedral
This unusual building is an unfinished cathedral in the Spanish city of Barcelon It was designed by a famous Spanish architect, Antonio Gaudí (1852–1926).

Bulls in the streets
Running from charging bulls is part of a festival held every July in the city of Pamplona. Hundreds of men run away from bulls that are let out in the streets.

Spanish dancing
The flamenco is a traditional dance with lots of twirling and stamping. It started in southern Spain about 500 years ago.

Paella
This traditional Spanish dish is mac from yellow rice mixed with seafood pieces of meat, tomatoes, and pepper

Which city held the 1992 Olympic Games?

Algarve beaches

Portugal's southern coast is called the Algarve. This warm area has many sandy beaches and it is a popular spot with holiday-makers from the rest of Europe.

The guitar is played by plucking the strings.

Classical guitar

Traditional Spanish music, including flamenco, is played on the classical guitar. The guitar was invented in Spain about 500 years ago.

Fishing industry

Bordered by the Atlantic Ocean and the Mediterranean Sea, Spain and Portugal have huge fishing industries. People who live on the coast eat lots of fish and seafood.

Lobsters turn red when they are cooked. Living lobsters are blue-grey.

A2307M

A2220.M

Traditional Portuguese fishing boats.

Barcelona.

Italy

Italy is shaped like a boot, with the top in the Alps mountains and the toe swimming in the Mediterranean Sea. The Apennine mountains run like a bone down the leg.

Italian lakes

There are 23 lakes in the lake district in northern Italy. Lake Garda is the biggest, and a popular place to sail and windsurf.

Skier

Dolomites

Lake Garda

Venice

Venetian gondola

River Po

Tagliatelli carbonara

San Marino

Mountain goat

Ferrari

Bologna

A l p s

Milan

Florence

Florence Cathedral

Wine

Leaning Tower of Pisa

Pisa

Turin

Fishing boat

Tuna

How many islands make up Malta?

N E S W

Italy

Octopus

Crab

Wine

Taranto

Olives and olive oil

Oranges

Sheep

Cast of a body at Pompeii

Almonds

▲ Mount Vesuvius
● **Pompeii**

Squid

Apennines

Vatican City

Pizza

Naples

Amalfi

Noto Cathedral

Messina

Scuba diving

ROME

The Colosseum (Rome)

Syracuse

Mount Etna

Can you find...

Europe's largest volcano?
Mount Etna in Sicily is also Europe's most active volcano.

The world's most wonky tower?
The Leaning Tower of Pisa is a campanile, or bell tower.

Where the first pizza was made? A baker in Naples invented the pizza in the 1800s.

Sicily

Palermo

Agrigento

Temple of Castor and Pollux

Malta

VALLETTA

Sardines

Sardinia

Tourism

Wild boar

● **Cagliari**

Lemons

Mediterranean Sea

Amalfi

Italy

Italy has some of the world's most beautiful cities, and its museums contain priceless paintings and sculptures. Italy also has modern industries, such as car-making and electronics.

Vatican City

The Vatican City is the home of the Pope, the head of the Roman Catholic Church. It is the world's smallest state and has its own flag.

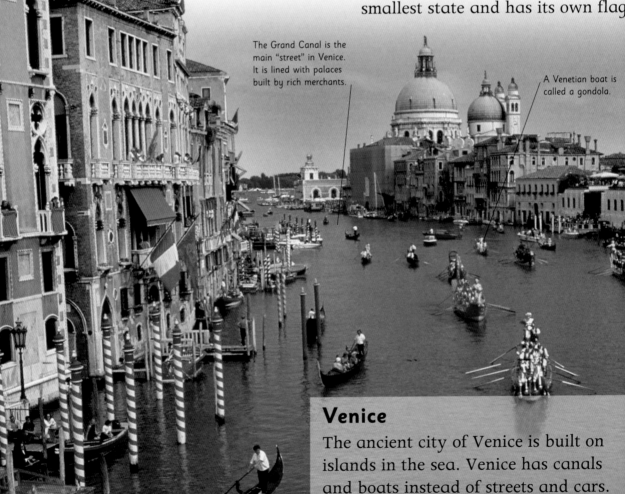

The Grand Canal is the main "street" in Venice. It is lined with palaces built by rich merchants.

A Venetian boat is called a gondola.

Venice

The ancient city of Venice is built on islands in the sea. Venice has canals and boats instead of streets and cars.

What were the people who lived in ancient Italy called?

Italian food

Italians enjoy eating with family and friends. Most meals include fresh vegetables and olive oil.

Cappuccino is coffee with frothy milk. Italians drink many different kinds of coffee.

Pasta is made in dozens of different shapes. This shape is called farfalle.

Ice cream has been made in Italy for more than 500 years.

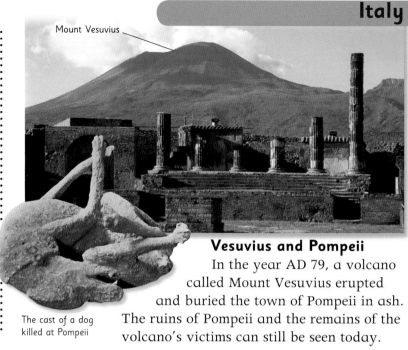

Mount Vesuvius

The cast of a dog killed at Pompeii

Vesuvius and Pompeii

In the year AD 79, a volcano called Mount Vesuvius erupted and buried the town of Pompeii in ash. The ruins of Pompeii and the remains of the volcano's victims can still be seen today.

Painted chapel

The Sistine Chapel is in the Vatican. It was painted about 500 years ago by great Italian painters, including the famous artist and sculptor Michelangelo.

Get going

Make a pizza from a piece of bread with some sliced tomatoes and cheese on top. Cook it under the grill or in the oven until the cheese melts.

It took Michelangelo four years to paint the ceiling of the Sistine Chapel, between 1508 and 1512.

Cars and scooters

Many famous makes of sports car come from Italy. This is a Ferrari. The streets of Italian towns and cities are full of buzzing scooters.

The Romans.

Central Eastern Europe

These countries were under communist rule until the 1990s. Today they are modern nations with thriving industries. Traditional farming continues in the rural areas.

Did you know?

The Polish town of Torun is well-known for its **gingerbread**.

Budapest is split by the Danube. Buda is on one bank, Pest on the other.

The snow-white **Lipizzaner horse** is bred in Slovenia.

Baltic Sea

Ship building

Gdansk

Koszalin

Szczecin

Windmills

Potato farming

Mining

Canoeing

Mazury lakes

European bison

Chemical industry

Torun

Gingerbread

Poznan

Pig farms

Wroclaw

River Oder

Poland

WARSAW

Market Square, Warsaw

River Vistula

Lublin

Sugar beet

Wheat

Kielce

Lodz

Cattle farms

Skiing

Germany

Charles Bridge

Karlovy Vary

PRAGUE

Hradec kralove

River Elbe

What ingredient makes Hungarian goulash spicy?

High Tatra Mountains

This mountain range lies in Poland and Slovakia, and forms part of the Carpathian Mountains. The tallest peak is 2,655 m (8,710 ft) high.

Romania

High Tatra Mountains

Spissky Hrad castle

Nyiregyhaza

Debrecen

Tokay wine

Parliament, Budapest

Szeged

Slovakia

Eger

Horses

BUDAPEST

River Danube

Hungary

Goulash

Pecs

Ostijek

Czech Republic

Brno

Wooden house

Painted Easter eggs

BRATISLAVA

Gyor

Croatia

ZAGREB

Dalmatian

Split

Skoda

Wine

LJUBLJANA

Slovenia

Dinaric Alps

Adriatic Sea

Dubrovnik

Austria

Rijeka

Tourism

Lipizzaner mare and foal

Pilsner lager

N
E
S
W

Paprika.

Central Eastern Europe

Winters bring deep snow to the plains and mountains of this part of Europe. Summers bring tourists to visit some of Europe's best preserved cities.

Vltava River, Prague

European bison

Old and modern

The capital of the Czech Republic is the historic city of Prague. It is full of ancient buildings because it has never been damaged by war.

Lake Bled bell
This is Lake Bled in Slovenia. Legend says that ringing the bell in the tower makes your wish come true.

Bison
About 1,000 wild bison live in Poland's forests. One of these enormous animals weighs as much as a family car.

Puppet performers
The Czechs love the theatre. Puppet theatre is especially popular here and in Slovakia.

What is the Czech word for "yes"?

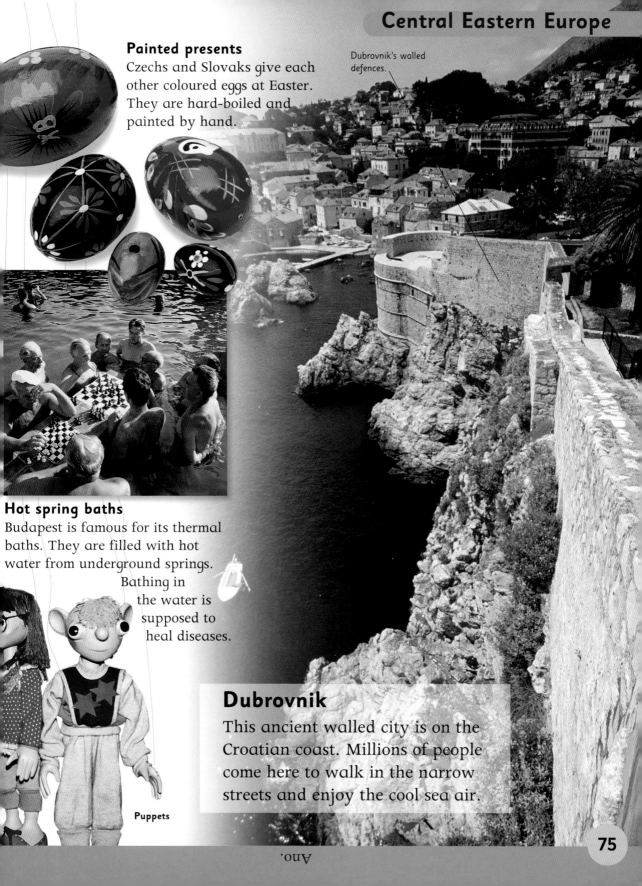

Painted presents

Czechs and Slovaks give each other coloured eggs at Easter. They are hard-boiled and painted by hand.

Dubrovnik's walled defences.

Hot spring baths

Budapest is famous for its thermal baths. They are filled with hot water from underground springs. Bathing in the water is supposed to heal diseases.

Puppets

Dubrovnik

This ancient walled city is on the Croatian coast. Millions of people come here to walk in the narrow streets and enjoy the cool sea air.

Eastern Europe

The countries of eastern Europe lie between the Baltic Sea and the Black Sea. They were part of the Soviet Union, but became independent states in 1991.

Hill of Crosses

This sacred site in Lithuania is visited by lots of pilgrims every year. They leave crosses on the hill to show their devotion to Christianity.

Russian Federation

Baltic Sea

Cruise ship

● TALLINN

Estonia

Golden eagle

Lake Peipus

Bison/Stag

Latvian costume

Amber jewellery
● Liepāja

Hill of Crosses

RIGA ●

Latvia

● Bauska

Trakai Castle

The centre of Europe

VILNIUS ●

Lithuania

Flax

Sugar beet

● Polatsk

● Vitsyebsk

Belarus

● MINSK

Poland

What are the Baltic States?

E N
W S

Coal mining
● Donets'k

● Kharkiv

White geese

● Dnipropetrovs'k

Sunflowers

Sea of Azov

● Kerch

River Dnieper

Crimea

● Yalta

St Andrew's Church

Black sea
tourism

Wheat

Swallow's
Nest
Castle

Black Sea

● Homyel

● Chernihiv

Mushroom
picking

● KIEV

Wooden church

● Chornobyl

Ukraine

Gymnastic
school

● Odesa

Mammoth fossils

● CHISINAU

Pripet Marshes

Mink

Moldova

Wooden Moldovian
gateway

Ukranian folk dancers

Potatoes

● L'viv

● Chernivtsi

Romania

Carpathian
Mountains

Can you find...

Ukraine's oldest creatures?
Mammoths walked the Earth
25,000 years ago.

The plant used to make linen?
Flax is a major crop of Belarus. Its
fibres are made into linen clothes.

Europe's largest marshland?
The Pripet Marshes cover 270,000
square kilometres (104,000 sq miles).

Estonia, Latvia, and Lithuania – the countries bordering the Baltic Sea.

stern Europe

The cold Baltic Sea makes Estonia, Latvia, and Lithuania damp and chilly. Ukraine is rich in natural resources such as oil, gas, coal, and metal ores.

The ancient city of Tallinn is Estonia's main port.

Rural life

Modern industries are growing in eastern Europe, but many people still live off the land. Farmers work with hand tools and horses rather than machines and tractors.

Estonian capital

Only a million people live in the hilly, wet country of Estonia. A third of them live in the capital, Tallinn.

Rhythmic gymnasts twirl ribbons and hoops as they leap about.

Luge tracks are covered in ice.

Latvian luge

Near Riga in Latvia is a huge bobsleigh and luge track used for international races. Competitors hurtle down it at up to 125 kph (78 mph).

Dancing gymnasts

Rhythmic gymnastics is a very popular sport in Ukraine. It is a combination of gymnastics and dance, set to music.

What is the world's most expensive caviar called?

Lithuanian amber

Amber is a kind of gem that forms over millions of years from conifer tree resin. Sometimes it has tiny creatures trapped inside it. Nearly all of the world's amber comes from mines in northern Lithuania.

This spider became trapped in amber millions of years ago.

Castle on the coast

One of the best known sights in southern Ukraine is Swallow's Nest Castle on the coast of Crimea. It used to be the home of a German oil tycoon but is now an Italian restaurant.

Swallow's Nest Castle is perched on a cliff overlooking the Black Sea.

Wolves

Grey wolves have been killed off in most of Europe, but packs of wolves still roam free in the Carpathian Mountains in southwestern Ukraine. They hunt wild boar and deer in mountain forests.

Traditional food

These are some of the traditional dishes eaten in Eastern Europe.

Draniki is made from potato pancakes stuffed with meat.

Caviar is an expensive delicacy made from the eggs of sturgeon fish.

Borsht is beetroot soup. It is eaten hold or cold.

Black Sea tourism

Many Eastern Europeans and Russians spend their summer holidays in Crimea, which has warm weather, miles of beaches, and dramatic, hilly scenery.

Almas caviar. It is shimmering white and costs £14,000 per kilogram.

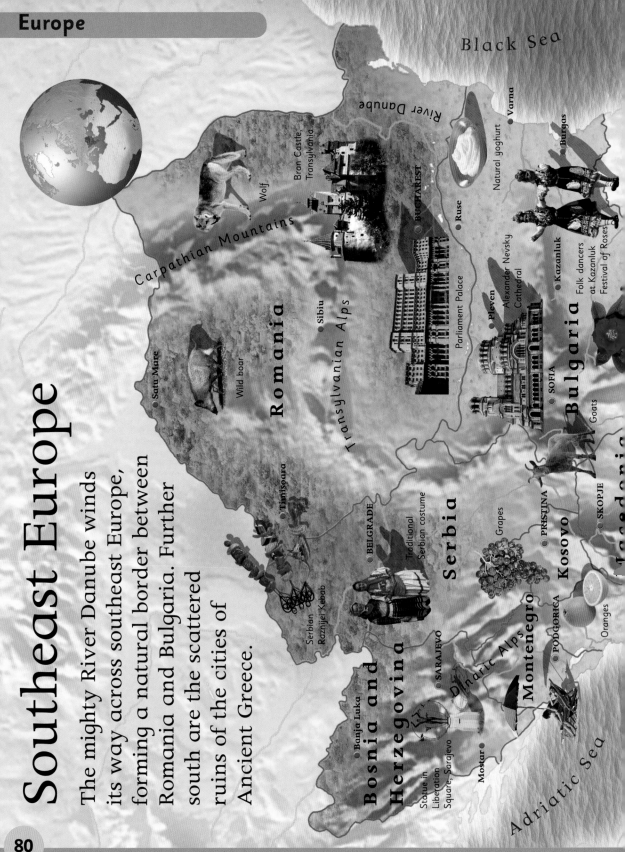

Southeast Europe

The mighty River Danube winds its way across southeast Europe, forming a natural border between Romania and Bulgaria. Further south are the scattered ruins of the cities of Ancient Greece.

Black Sea

River Danube

Varna

Burgas

Natural yoghurt

Wolf

Bran Castle, Transylvania

BUCHAREST

Ruse

Alexander Nevsky Cathedral

Kazanluk

Folk dancers at Kazanluk Festival of Roses

Carpathian Mountains

Pleven

Parliament Palace

Sibiu

Romania

SOFIA

Bulgaria

Satu Mare

Transylvanian Alps

Goats

Wild boar

Timișoara

BELGRADE

Traditional Serbian costume

Serbia

Grapes

PRISTINA

SKOPJE

Kosovo

Macedonia

Serbian Raznjiei Kebab

PODGORICA

Montenegro

Oranges

Banja Luka

SARAJEVO

Dinaric Alps

Bosnia and Herzegovina

Statue in Liberation Square, Sarajevo

Mostar

Adriatic Sea

Turkey

N
E
W
S

Rhodes

Sponge

Dolphins

Lesbos

Chios

Aegean Sea

Cyclades Islands

Knossos Palace

● Irâklion
Crete

ATHENS

Ceremonial soldier
from Athens

● Salonika

Olive oil

Greece

Parthenon

Pindus Mountains

Greek coffee

Greek vase

● Patras
Peloponnese

Greek church

Mediterranean Sea

...ania

Cephalonia

Zakinthos

Watermelon

Octopus

Sailing ship

Can you find...

A sponge? Old-fashioned bathroom sponges are the skeletons of dead sea creatures.

Yoghurt? People in Bulgaria eat lots of yoghurt because they think it helps them live longer.

Greek coffee? Greek people make coffee by boiling ground coffee in a tiny pan of water until it foams.

Chios Island in the Aegean Sea

Olives.

Southeast Europe

Southeast Europe is hot and hilly, with miles of sunny beaches. Many of the people are farmers, but the tourism is also important. People from all over the world visit Greece to see its ancient ruins and visit its islands.

Greek soldiers
This soldier is called an Evzone. He is a guard at the Greek parliament building in Athens.

Food

Many crops are grown in this part of Europe.

Grapes for making wine grow well in the warm climate.

Watermelons are refreshing fruits that grow on the ground.

Maize is grown for flour, animal food, and as a fuel.

White-washed churches dot the sunny islands of Greece.

The Parthenon
This ancient temple stands on a rocky outcrop in the centre of Athens. It was built nearly 2,500 years ago.

Greek islands

Greece has more than 2,000 sun-baked islands. Millions of Europeans come here on holiday.

What major sporting tournament began in Greece in 776 BC?

Bran Castle,
Transylvania

Rose festival

Bulgarian farmers grow roses for making perfume. About 2,000 petals are needed to make just one gram of rose-oil. The rose-pickers hold a festival every year at harvest time.

Rose-picking festival in June at Kazanluk, Bulgaria

The legend of Dracula

Transylvania is a region in the north of Romania. The mountains here are covered with forests. Transylvania was the home of a vampire in the novel *Dracula*.

Goat farming

Farming is hard work in the dry heat of Greece. Many farmers keep a herd of goats for cheese and milk.

Dancing gypsy

Southeast Europe has many Romany people (gypsies). They spend their lives travelling, and they love traditional music and dance.

The Olympic Games.

Russia and Central Asia

The Russian Federation spans two continents:
Europe and Asia. To its southwest are the
eight independent countries of
Central Asia and Caucasia.

Barents Sea

Murmansk

Icebreaker
ship

Harp seal

Kara Sea

Kaliningrad

St Petersburg

Pskov

Novgorod

Kirov ballet

Vorkuta

Noril'sk

St Basil's Cathedral,
Moscow

MOSCOW

Kirov

Ural Mountains

River Ob

S i

Russian dolls

River Volga

Chess

Ural'sk

Magnitogorsk

River Ob

Elk

Black Sea

Orsk

Omsk

Novosibirsk

R u s s i a n

Georgia

Caucasus

Groznyy

Sturgeon
fish caviar

Baykonur
Space Centre

ASTANA

Wheat

T'BILISI

Baykonur

YEREVAN

Aral Sea

Zhezkazgan

Armenia

Azerbaijan

Kazakhstan

BAKU

Uzbekistan

Lake Balkhash

Caspian
Sea

Turkmenistan

Kyzyl Kum
Desert

Cotton

Iran

ASHGABAT

Samarqand

TASHKENT

BISHKEK

Almaty

Gur-Emir Mausoleum,
Samarqand

Kyrgyzstan

DUSHANBE

Tajikistan

Afghanistan

Where is 90 per cent of Russia's tea grown?

Arctic Ocean

Brent geese

Pevek

Walrus

Reindeer

Nenet people

Yakut people

River Lena

Verkhoyansk

Wolf

Magadan

r i a

Yakutsk

Okhotsk

Kamchatka Peninsula

Sea of Okhotsk

Walkabout
Russia is the world's widest country. It would take more than two months to cross if you walked non-stop from west to east.

Salmon

Brown bear

N

W E

S

Diamonds

Timber

Mining

Federation

Bratsk

Trans-Siberian railway

Khabarovsk

Irkutsk

Lake Baikal

Siberian tiger

Did you know?

Caviar from the Caspian Sea is so expensive it is known as "black gold".

Lake Baikal is the world's deepest, and largest, freshwater lake.

Verkhoyansk is the world's coldest town. In winter the temperature falls to -68°C (-90°F).

Freshwater seal

China

Vladivostok

A shrinking sea
The Aral Sea, between Kazakhstan and Uzbekistan, is shrinking. The water is being used on Uzbekistan's cotton fields, stranding fishing boats.

Georgia.

Russia

Russia is the world's largest country. Most people live in cities in the west, near the rest of Europe. Russia is governed from Moscow.

Russian churches have domed roofs shaped like onions.

The Summer Palace

This magnificent palace is in St Petersburg. It was built 300 years ago for Peter the Great, who was the ruler, or tsar, of Russia.

St Basil's

St Basil's Cathedral is in Red Square, Moscow. Churches are important to Russians. Three-quarters of Russians follow the Russian Orthodox branch of Christianity.

Russian dolls fit inside each other.

What was St Petersburg called when Russia was in the Soviet Union?

Ballet school

The Bolshoi Ballet is Russia's most famous ballet company. Dancers trained at its ballet school perform at the Bolshoi Theatre in Moscow.

Russian culture

Culture is very important in Russia, especially music, art, theatre, and literature.

Tchaikovsky and **Stravinsky**, both famous composers, were born in Russia.

The Russian writer **Tolstoy** wrote the famous novel *War and Peace*.

The **balalaika** is a traditional Russian instrument. It is played by plucking its strings.

Soviet Russia

Russia once belonged to a huge federation called the Soviet Union. The Kremlin in Moscow was its seat of government.

The Kremlin is an enormous fortress in Moscow.

The red star, hammer, and sickle were the symbols of the Soviet Union.

Brown bear

The brown bear is the symbol of Russia. It lives in the north, hunting fish and small animals.

Vladimir Ilyich Lenin (1870–1924) was the leader who founded the Soviet Union.

Siberia and neighbours

Siberia is a vast area of pine forests to the east of the Ural mountains. Northern Siberia is so cold that the ground is frozen all year round.

Tents of Siberian reindeer herders

Reindeer
This ivory carving from Siberia shows a reindeer pulling a sledge. People in northern Siberia keep reindeer for milk, meat, and fur, as well as for pulling sledges.

Siberian people

The Nenets live in the forests of Siberia in winter. In summer they pack up their tents and travel north with reindeer herds to pasture in the Arctic.

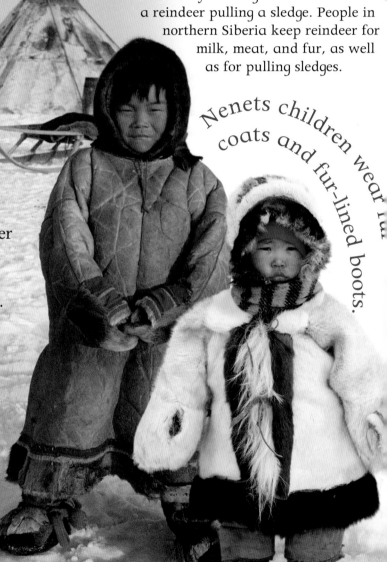

Nenets children wear fur coats and fur-lined boots.

The Trans-Siberian railway
It takes eight days to travel from Moscow to Vladivostok along the Trans-Siberian railway. It's the longest railway line in the world.

How long is the Trans-Siberian railway?

Made in Russia

Here are some of the well-known objects made by Russia's craftspeople.

A **samovar** is a decorated urn for heating water for tea.

Antique jewellery **Fabergé eggs** are worth a fortune.

Clay dolls have been made for the Dymkovo village fair for many years.

Warm **boots** are made from the furs of Siberian forest animals.

Many Russian **toys** were traditionally carved from wood.

Oil in Azerbaijan

There is a lot of oil, gas, coal, and other materials under the ground in Azerbaijan in Central Asia. Azerbaijan gets most of its money by selling oil.

Russian Rockets

Baykonur Space Centre in Kazakhstan is the home of Russia's space programme, and where they launch their rockets. Sputnik, the first man-made space satellite, was launched here in 1957.

Rockets lift off from Baykonur Space Centre.

The top of the rocket carries a satellite or supplies for astronauts already in space.

Engines push the rocket upwards.

Weaving carpets

Central Asian women weave decorative woollen carpets to give as wedding presents. The carpets are made by hand and coloured with plant dyes.

9,440 km (5,870 miles).

Middle East

This part of the world is hot and dry, with large deserts. Three of the world's great religions began here.

Istanbul

Blue Mosque   ANK

Turkey

Mediterranean Sea

NIC
Cypru

Sculp
meno
Jerus

Mecca

The holiest place for a Muslim is the Ka'ba, a cube-shaped shrine in Mecca. Muslims face the Ka'ba when they pray and try to visit it at least once in their lifetime.

World's first skyscrapers

The people of Yemen started building mud-brick skyscrapers thousands of years ago. The ground floors are used for animals or for storing goods. Families live in the upper floors.

Fruits of the desert

Farmers can grow crops only in the wettest parts of the Middle East.

Figs are soft, sticky fruits that can be dried to make them last longer.

Olives are grown for their seeds, which are pressed to make olive oil.

Dates are the fruit of palm trees, which grow by rivers and in oases.

Which country produces 65 per cent of the world's hazelnuts?

Black Sea

irling
vish dancer

Head of Zeus

Mount Ararat
5,165 m ▲
(16,945 ft)

Caspian Sea

Syria

Olives

Figs

TEHRAN

Turquoise

RUT

Lebanon

DAMASCUS

Chador, traditional
dress for women

Iran

AMMAN

SALEM

Jordan

Iraq

BAGHDAD

Iranian food – chicken kebab

Marsh Arab reed house

Falconry

Kuwait

KUWAIT
CITY

The Gulf

Bahrain

Persepolis palace

Ancient city
of Petra

Desert
oasis

Qatar

Oman

Gulf of Oman

ABU DHABI

DOHA

RIYADH

Oil

United
Arab Emirates

MUSCAT

Red Sea

Mecca

Saudi Arabia

Oil refinery

Mecca

Arabian desert

Oman

oral reefs grow
ong the coast
the Red Sea,
here the water
warm and clear.

Camels

Desert oryx

Oil tanker

N

W

E

Yemen

SANA

Frankincense tree

Arabian Sea

S

Middle East

The Middle East lies at the crossroads between Europe, Africa, and Asia. Most of the people are Muslims — followers of the religion of Islam.

Middle Eastern treat

Baklava is a popular Middle Eastern pastry. It is made from rolled layers of thin pastry and chopped nuts, covered with sticky honey.

The towers around a mosque are called minarets. This is the Blue Mosque in Istanbul, Turkey.

Mosques

Muslims pray in buildings called mosques. Mosques are decorated with patterned tiles and verses from the Muslim holy book, the Qur'an.

Patterned Islamic tile

Traditional dress

Muslim women hide their hair and the shape of their body with loose-fitting clothes when they go out in public.

Camels can last for ten months

Camel train carrying cargo across the desert

What language is spoken in most of the Middle East?

The Western Wall

Jerusalem is a holy city for Muslims, Christians, and Jews. Jews pray at the Western Wall. It is the only part that is left of a Jewish temple that was built 2,000 years ago.

Salty sea

The Dead Sea is 400 metres (1,300 ft) below sea level. It is so salty that people can float in the water. Plants and animals cannot survive in it.

Oil wealth

More than half the world's oil lies under the ground in the Middle East. The discovery of oil and gas has made many of the countries in the Middle East very rich. They sell lots of oil to other countries, some of which is turned into petrol for cars.

Burj Al-Arab hotel in Dubai, United Arab Emirates

World's tallest hotel

The Burj-Al-Arab hotel in Dubai is the world's tallest hotel. It was built on an artificial island and designed to look like the sail of a ship.

Get going

Make an Arab headdress. Fold a chequered tablecloth diagonally in half and hang it over your head, leaving your face clear. Then tie it in place with a dark belt or ribbon.

Arab men wear long, baggy clothes and a headdress to shade them from the hot desert sun.

vithout a drink of water.

Southern Asia

Southern Asia is colourful and crowded. India is the biggest country in the region, with a population of more than a billion.

Elephants on parade

During the festival of Puram in southern India, 101 elephants march through the town of Trichur in a grand parade.

Snow leopard

Lapis lazuli

Herat

Afghanistan

Decorated lorry

KABUL

Quetta

ISLAMABAD

Pakistan

Multan

Tomb of Muhammad Ali Jinnah

Golden Temple

Dancer

Hyderabad

Karachi

Taj Mahal

Delhi
NEW DELHI

Agra

India

Rickshaw

Camel market

Green turtles

Nepal

River Ganges

River dolphin

Tea picking

Imphal

Bangladesh

DHAKA

When Hindus die, where are their ashes scattered?

Coconut tree and coconut

Andaman Islands (India)

Nicobar Islands (India)

Bay of Bengal

Fishing boat

Cuttack

Common lobster

Herring

N

E

W

S

Tiger

Vijayawada

Thresher shark

Chennai (Madras)

Sri Lanka

Jaffna

Kandy

Tea leaves

Mumbai (Bombay)

Snake charmer

Kathkali Dancer

COLOMBO

Indian elephant

Calicut

Trichur

Arabian Sea

Tuna fish

Can you find...

Lapis lazuli? This precious stone was once used to make brilliant, sky-blue paint.

An Indian dancer? Classical dancers use movements of their bodies to tell ancient stories.

Ganges river dolphin? This dolphin is almost blind and finds its way in muddy water by sound.

The Monsoon

Southern Asia is normally hot and dry, but every summer it pours down for weeks. This rainy season, called the monsoon, helps farmers grow crops like rice.

In the River Ganges.

Southern Asia

Different cultures and religions mix together in Southern Asia. Most people are Hindus, but there are also Muslims, Buddhists, Sikhs, and Christians.

Indian food

Spicy chicken

Dumplings

Vegetables

Lentil soup

Bread

Rice

Raita (yoghurt dip)

Poppadoms

Traditional Indian meals consist of lots of separate dishes on a metal plate called a thali.

Pilgrims bathing in the Ganges

Disappearing tigers

Tigers once lived all over southern Asia, but today they are rare because of hunting. Parts of India and Bangladesh still have man-eating tigers.

Four minarets surround the central tomb.

Indian arts

Indian people enjoy music, dance, theatre, and story telling. In the art of Kathakali, dancers act out Hindu myths.

Kathakali dancer

The Holy Ganges

The River Ganges is sacred to Hindus. They believe that the river's water washes away their sins. Millions of pilgrims bathe at the holy city of Varanasi.

What is the main crop in Sri Lanka?

Bollywood

So many films are made in Bombay (Mumbai) that people call this town Bollywood. Indian films are very long and feature lots of singing and dancing.

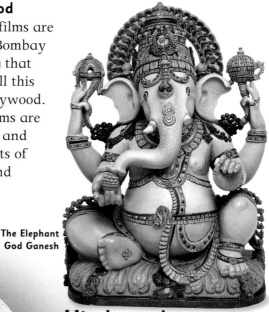

The Elephant God Ganesh

Taj Mahal

The Taj Mahal is a tomb. An Indian emperor called Shah Jahan built it more than 300 years ago for his favourite wife when she died.

Hindu gods

Hindus worship many gods. Statues of Ganesh, the elephant god, are placed near entrances to houses.

Get going

Make some raita (Indian yoghurt dip). Put some plain yoghurt in a small dish. Grate some cucumber and mix it into the yoghurt. Add a sprinkling of coriander leaves or mint.

Tea.

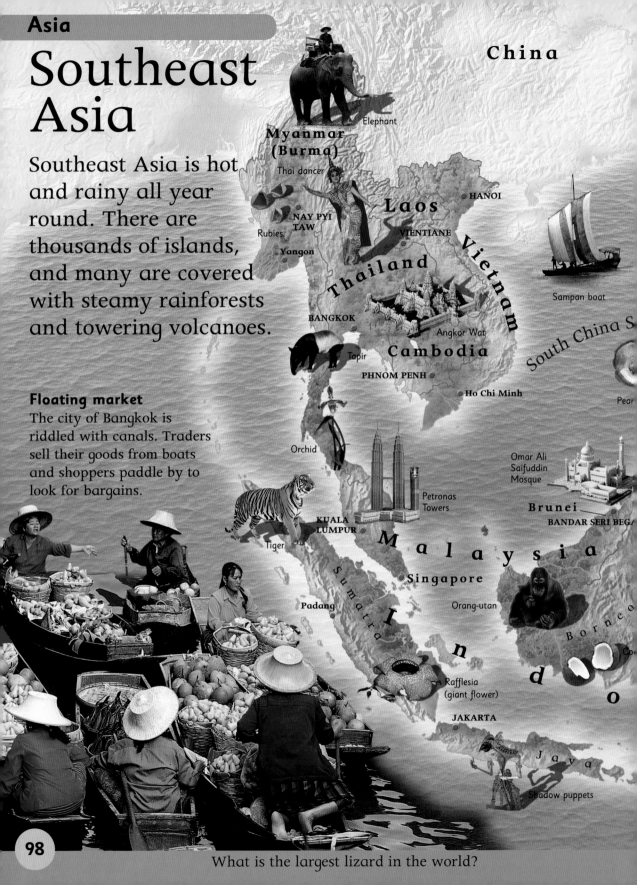

Southeast Asia

Southeast Asia is hot and rainy all year round. There are thousands of islands, and many are covered with steamy rainforests and towering volcanoes.

China

Elephant

Myanmar (Burma)

Thai dancer

NAY PYI TAW

Rubies

Yangon

Laos

HANOI

VIENTIANE

Thailand

Vietnam

Sampan boat

BANGKOK

Angkor Wat

Tapir

Cambodia

PHNOM PENH

Ho Chi Minh

South China S

Pear

Floating market
The city of Bangkok is riddled with canals. Traders sell their goods from boats and shoppers paddle by to look for bargains.

Orchid

Petronas Towers

Omar Ali Saifuddin Mosque

Brunei

BANDAR SERI BEGA

KUALA LUMPUR

Tiger

M a l a y s i a

Singapore

Orang-utan

Sumatra

B o r n e o

Padang

I n

Rafflesia (giant flower)

o

JAKARTA

J a v a

Shadow puppets

98

Can you find...

A very rare kind of ape? **Orang-utans** live only in Borneo and Sumatra.

An animal with tusks that grow through its face? The **babirusa** is a kind of pig.

The world's largest flower? **Rafflesia** grows to nearly a metre (3 feet) wide.

Planting rice

ANILA

Vinta boats

Philippines

Cebu

Water buffalo

Davao

Pacific Ocean

Celebes Sea

Tuna

Rice paddies

The wet climate is ideal for growing rice. Farmers plant it in flooded fields called paddies, which are sometimes built like steps in the sides of hills.

Babirusa

Moluccas

Nutmeg

Ambon

Celebes

Toraja house

e s i a

New Guinea

Jayapura

Conch shell

Asmat warrior

Papua New Guinea

Komodo dragon

DILI
East Timor

Mangoes

PORT MORESBY

The Komodo dragon. It can grow to 3 m (10 ft) long.

99

Southeast Asia

The 10 countries of Southeast Asia are spread over islands and mainland. The smallest is the island state of Singapore. The biggest is Indonesia, which has more than 13,000 islands.

Reclining Buddha

Many Southeast Asians are Buddhist. Their religion was founded by a man called the Buddha 2,500 years ago. Statues of reclining Buddha show him on his death-bed.

Reclining Buddha in Ayuthaya, Thailand   Buddhist monk

Temple in the jungle

The magnificent temple of Angkor Wat in Cambodia was built 900 years ago. It was hidden by overgrown jungle until archaeologists cleared the trees last century.

Angkor Wat's towers are shown on Cambodia's national flag.

New Guinea

Hundreds of tribes live among the jungle-covered mountains of New Guinea, and many have a unique language. This girl is from the Mount Hagen tribe.

What smelly fruit is banned from many restaurants in Southeast Asia?

Exotic Fruit

Tropical fruits grow well in Southeast Asia's warm, wet climate.

 The **durian** tastes delicious but smells disgusting.

 Inside a **coconut** is white flesh and a hole filled with liquid.

 The **custard apple** has cream-coloured flesh like thick custard.

 Slices of **starfruit** make star-shaped decorations for puddings.

 The **rambutan** has a tough skin covered with soft hairs.

The Petronas Towers

These office blocks in Kuala Lumpur, Malaysia, were the world's tallest buildings from 1998 until 2003. Each tower is 452 m (1,483 ft) tall.

Island wildlife

Many extraordinary animals and plants live in Southeast Asia. Orang-utans live in rainforests on Borneo and Sumatra. Komodo dragons are flesh-eating lizards found on a few islands in Indonesia.

Long-necked women

The Karen tribe live in the hills of Burma. The women stretch their necks as they grow up by wearing neck rings.

Orang-utans swing on flimsy trees and branches to move through the forest.

Komodo dragon

The durian.

China and neighbours

Over 1 billion people live in China – that's one-fifth of the world's people. Next door, Mongolia has the fewest people for its size.

Terracotta Army

This army of statues in Xi'an was made more than 2,000 years ago to guard the tomb of Qin Shi Huang, China's first emperor. The statues were rediscovered in 1974.

Chinese opera

Chinese opera has lots of singing, acting, and acrobatics. Make-up is used to show the type of character being played.

Altay

Mongoli ger (hous

Yining

Urumqi

Ba car

Turpan

Har

Kashi

Ibex

K2

Yak

Tibet

Potala Palace

Bhairabnath Temple

Lh

KATHMANDU
Mount Everest

Nepal

THIN
Bhuta

Can you find...

The world's tallest mountain? Mount Everest is 8,850 metres (29,035 ft) tall.

The world's most crowded place? Hong Kong has 6,000 people per square kilometre (2,300 per square mile).

China's hottest place? Turpan has recorded temperatures of up to 47°C (117°F).

What is the world's second-tallest mountain?

Russian Federation

Mongolia

● ULAN BATOR

Dinosaur fossils

Gobi Desert

Snow sculptures at the
Harbin Ice Festival

●Harbin

●Jinlin

●Shenyang

North Korea

●PYONGYANG

Temple of Heaven

Dalian

●BEIJING

SEOUL

**South
Korea**

Seoul Olympic
Stadium

Qingdao

Korea
Strait

C h i n a

Great Wall of China

Yellow River

●Lanzhou

●Xi'an

Tea plantation

Tibetan
monk

●Shanghai

**East China
Sea**

Hanzhou

River Yangtze

Wuhan

Junk (fishing boat)

Chengdu ●

China porcelain

●Changsha

Silk moth

Fuzhou

●Taipei

T a i w a n

Hong Kong business district
and Exhibition Centre

Electronic
goods

Red panda

Kunming ●

Giant panda

Hong Kong

Nanning

Hainan

South China Sea

K2 in the Himalayas. It is 8,611 metres (28,250 ft) tall.

103

Eastern China and Korea

China is a vast and ancient country. Emperors ruled it for thousands of years, but today it has a communist government. Korea is split into two countries: North Korea and South Korea.

Packed Hong Kong

Hong Kong is a small and crowded region of China. It is an important centre for banking and commerce.

Staple food

Rice is the main crop, and the most important source of food, in China and Korea. Eastern China's rainy climate is ideal for rice, which grows best in flooded fields.

Rice is eaten with chopsticks.

Rice farm

Great Wall

More than 500 years ago, the Chinese built the Great Wall of China to keep out invaders from Mongolia. It is the longest man-made structure in the world.

On your bike

There are millions of bicycles in China, especially in rural areas. In cities such as Beijing there are more cars. Bicycles are also used as taxis and market stalls.

What are Chinese years named after?

Martial arts

Chinese and Korean people have turned fighting into an art form. One of the most popular martial arts in Korea is tae kwon do, which is used for self-defence or sport. Kicking and punching are allowed.

Tae kwon do fighters

The misty Guilin mountains are said to be the most beautiful place in China.

Chinese New Year

The most important festival in China is the Chinese New Year, when people celebrate the return of spring. One of the main events is a parade led by a huge dancing dragon.

Guilin Mountains

The town of Guilin in southern China is surrounded by small, pointy mountains that are often shrouded in mist. They are a favourite subject for Chinese painters.

The Chinese dragon is a symbol of strength and good luck.

Himalayas and Western China

The Himalayas are the tallest mountains on Earth, yet many people live among them. North of the mountains are the cold, dusty highlands of western China and Mongolia.

Monks and prayer wheels

Tibetan monks

In Tibet, Buddhist monks start their training as young boys. They shave their heads, wear red robes, and join a monastery for life.

The Himalayan peaks are always snowy.

The Himalayas stretch for 2,500 km (1,550 miles).

Mountain villages

In Nepal, villages are dotted about in valleys between the highest mountains. Farmers build flat terraces in the hillsides for growing crops.

Who is the Dalai Lama?

Mongolian horsemen

Mongolians learn to ride by the age of three. Many spend their lives on the move, riding across Mongolia's vast plains with herds of horses and sheep.

Mongolian horse-riding festival

Climbing Everest

The ultimate challenge for a mountaineer is to climb Mount Everest, the world's tallest mountain. Dozens of people reach the summit every year, but some die on the way.

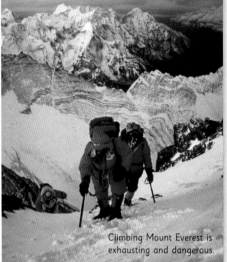

Climbing Mount Everest is exhausting and dangerous.

Buddhist prayer flags

Get going

Make Buddhist prayer flags. Attach squares of coloured tissue to a length of string. Hang the string across your room or a garden.

Potala Palace

In the town of Lhasa in Tibet stands a mighty fortress called Potala Palace. It used to be the headquarters of the Tibetan government before Tibet became a part of China.

The useful yak

A yak is kind of huge, shaggy cow that can survive in the cold, thin mountain air. Tibetan people get milk, butter, meat, and wool from yaks.

Basket hangs on back.

Cheese sellers

These Tibetan girls are nomads, which means they move from place to place. They are selling dried yak's cheese.

The head of Tibetan Buddhism and the leader of Tibet's people.

Japan

Japan is made up of four large islands and several thousand small ones. Most of the country is mountainous. The biggest cities are near the coast, where the land is flat.

Kurile Islands

Steller's sea eagle

Hokkaido

Japanese crane

Sapporo

Pollack

Snow monkey

Aomori

Apples

Ou Mountains

Sushi

Cups for rice wine

Honshu

Sea of Japan

N
E
S
W

Snow and ice festival

An ice festival takes place every February in the town of Sapporo. People carve towers of ice into temples, sculptures, or replicas of famous buildings.

How many people live in Tokyo?

Robot dog

Toys and gadgets
Japan makes lots of electronic goods, such as computer games, televisions, and robot pets.

Ogasawara Islands

Volcano Islands

Kabuki theatre

Izu Islands

Pearl in shell

Mount Fuji 3,776 m (12,388 ft)

Nagoya Castle

Nagoya

Pacific Ocean

Kyoto ● **Osaka**

Geisha

Chugoku Mountains

Bullet train

Tokyo skyline
The capital city Tokyo is crowded and lively. Its skyscrapers are designed to sway slightly, which protects them from falling during earthquakes.

Shikoku

● **Hiroshima**

Matsuyama castle

Sumo wrestlers

Shinto shrine

Oki Islands

Kyushu

Iki

Fukuoka ●

Pottery

Bonsai tree

Nagasaki ●

Octopus

East China Sea

Ryukyu islands

Sakishima Islands
These small tropical islands lie far to the south of the rest of Japan.

Ishigaki

Iriomote

● **Yonaguni**

Okinawa

Japan

Japan is a fascinating mixture of old and new. Its people work very hard and have made Japan very wealthy.

Cherry blossom

Mount Fuji

Mount Fuji

This snow-capped volcano is the symbol of Japan, and many Japanese people have a picture of it in their homes. Mount Fuji last erupted in 1707.

Bullet trains

Japanese "bullet trains" are among the fastest trains in the world. They shoot between cities at up to 270 kph (167 mph).

Snow monkeys

Japanese macaques stay warm in winter by bathing in hot springs. These clever monkeys have also learnt how to make snowballs.

Volcano protection

Volcanoes and earthquakes are common in Japan. In the city of Kagoshima, children wear helmets to protect them from rocks and ash from nearby Mount Sakurajima.

What do Japanese people call their country?

Traditional dress

On special occasions, women and girls wear a kimono – a richly embroidered silk dress tied with a sash.

Cherry blossom

The national flower of Japan is the cherry blossom. In spring, people celebrate the arrival of the cherry blossom with picnics under the trees.

Sumo

Traditional Japanese wrestling is called sumo. The heavy wrestlers try to throw each other out of the ring, called the dohyo.

Thick belt called a mawashi.

Open shoes called zori.

Buddhist temple

Japan's two main religions are Buddhism and Shinto. Buddhist temples, or pagodas, consist of a stack of wooden floors and curved roofs. Ornate gardens often surround them.

Chopsticks

Sushi

Japanese people eat a lot of seafood. Sushi consists of small snacks of rice, raw fish, and vegetables.

111

Australia

Australia is the world's smallest continent, but it is a huge country. Most Australians live on the coast, far from the vast, dusty deserts that make up the outback.

Poisonous animals

More poisonous animals live in Australia than in any other country.

The male **platypus** has a poisonous spur on each of its back ankles.

A **box jellyfish's** stings can kill and cause terrible pain that lasts for weeks.

Taipans are the world's deadliest snakes. A bite can kill in 30 minutes.

Sea snake venom can kill a child, but bites from these shy snakes are rare.

Cone shells are sea snails with deadly stings. The venom causes suffocation.

Funnel-web spiders can bite through a fingernail and stop a person's heart.

The tiny **blue-ringed octopus** can paralyse and kill a person with its bite.

Darwin

Saltwater crocodile

Boomerang

Broome

Dingo

Tanami Desert

Great Sandy Desert

Northern Territory

Port Hedland

Emu

Iron ore

Road train

Musgra

Camel

Western Australia

Great Victoria Desert

Sout Austra

Geraldton

Kalgoorlie

Perth skyline

Perth

Fremantle

Kangaroo

Great Australian Big

Esperance

Great white shark

Albany

N

W   E

S

112

What is a coral reef made from?

Aboriginal paintings

Gulf of Carpentaria

Cape York Peninsula

Cairns

Coral reef

The Great Barrier Reef stretches for 2,000 km (1,200 miles) along Queensland's coast. Many brightly coloured fish live on the reef.

ant Creek

The Devils Marbles

Mount Isa

Cattle farms

Townsville

Mackay

Great Barrier Reef

Flying doctor

Queensland

Rainbow lorikeet

Rockhampton

ce Springs

Great Dividing Range

mpson Desert

ru (Ayer's Rock)

Sheep stations

Koala

nges

Lake Eyre

Opals
oober Pedy

Banana plantations

Pineapple farms

Brisbane

Broken Hill

Funnel-web spider

Sydney Opera House

rt Augusta

New South Wales

Sydney

Whyalla

Wollongong

Kookaburra

Wagga Wagga

Port Lincoln

Adelaide

Murray river

CANBERRA

Australian Capital Territory

Kangaroo Island

Victoria

Melbourne

Mount Gambier

Tram

Bass Strait

Tasmanian devil

Tasmania

Hobart

Sailing

The skeletons of tiny sea creatures.

Australia

Australia is on the opposite side of the world from Europe, but most Australians are descended from European settlers. English is the main language in Australia.

Australian shepherds use jeeps to round up their enormous flocks.

Australian Aborigines

The Aborigines have lived in Australia for more than 50,000 years. According to their legends, the world was made by mythical beasts who carved the land into rivers and mountains.

Sheep farms

About a quarter of the world's wool comes from Australia. Some sheep farms are so remote that farmers need planes to visit town.

Boomerangs fly back to you after you throw them.

A boomerang is a throwing weapon that Aborigines use for hunting.

What is the capital of Australia?

Gum trees (eucalyptus trees) have waxy, strong-smelling leaves.

Sydney
Australia's biggest city and chief port is Sydney. Its most famous building is Sydney Opera House in the harbour. Around Sydney are miles of beaches where children can swim and surf after school.

Koala
The only animal that can eat the leaves of Australia's gum trees is the koala. Koalas are very lazy and spend up to 20 hours a day sleeping.

Get going
Make an Aboriginal lucky stone. Find a smooth, round pebble and paint a pattern of lines and dots on it to make a picture of an imaginary creature.

On the beach
In Australia, the seasons are the other way round. December is the middle of summer, so Australians celebrate Christmas on the beach.

Bouncing babies
Kangaroos are marsupials – they carry their babies in a pouch. Lots of Australian animals are marsupials.

Kangaroos move by hopping on their huge back feet.

Uluru
Uluru, or Ayers Rock, is a huge lump of sandstone rock in the centre of Australia. Aborigines believe it is a magical place.

New Zealand
and the Pacific

Hundreds of islands are scattered across the Pacific Ocean. Two of the biggest form the mountainous country of New Zealand.

Extreme sports
New Zealand is the world capital for extreme sports. Bungee jumping, sky divin and white-water rafting are all popular.

Maori war dance
Most people in New Zealand are European, but about one in ten are Maoris – New Zealand's native people. On special occasions, Maoris paint their faces and perform a war dance called a haka.

Moving house
Earthquakes are common in New Zealand, so people live in wooden houses for safety. When people move home, they can carry their house away on a lorry.

Sheep she

Kiwi

South Island

Mount Cook

Christchurch

Southern Alps

Takahe

Rugby

Queenstown

N e

Dunedin

Bungee jumping

Royal albatross

Sheep

Oysters

What's unusual about New Zealand's kiwi birds?

Red snapper

N
W E
S

Auckland

Pohuto geyser

Pacific
Ocean

Maori carving Kiwi fruit

North Island

Parliament buildings
(Wellington)

WELLINGTON

Z e a l a n d

Coconut palms
Forests of coconut palms
grow along the beaches
of the Pacific islands.
Islanders climb these tall
trees to gather the coconuts.

Pacific islands

About 5 million people live
among the tropical islands
of the central Pacific.

Northern Mariana
Islands (US)

Marshall
Islands

Guam (US)

erm
ale

Palau Micronesia

Papua New Nauru
Guinea

Kiribati

Solomon Tuvalu
Islands

Tokelau (NZ)

Wallis & American
Futuna Samoa Samoa
(France) (US)

Pacific
islanders fish from
small wooden
canoes.

Vanuatu

Tonga Niue Cook Islands
(NZ) (NZ)

New
Caledonia
(France)

Fiji

French
Polynesia
(France)

Antarctica

The world's coldest continent is Antarctica, which is covered in ice. In winter it doubles in size as the sea freezes around it.

Adélie penguins

Penguins

Lots of sea animals live around Antarctica's coast. Penguins are clumsy on land but superb swimmers underwater.

A signpost in Antarctica shows how far away the rest of the world is.

NORTH POLE 11708 MI.

CHRISTCHURCH 2457 MI.

SEATTLE WASH. 9,942 MI.

QUONSET PT. 10,598 MI.

ST. PAUL MINN. 10,002 MI.

SOUTH POLE 831 MI.

SALINAS, CAL. 8,777 MI.

HOUSTON TEXAS 9141 MI.

MOBILE ALA. 9641 MI.

PONTIAC MICH. 10,249 MI.

ERECTED BY YX-6 OF 3" WINTERING PARTY 1958 THEY WENT THAT-A-WAY ➤➤

Scott and the Antarctic

The British explorer Robert Scott was one of the first people to reach the South Pole, in 1912. He died of cold and hunger on the way home.

Southern Ocean

Antarctic Peninsula

South polar skua

Weddell Sea

Halley Research Station (UK)

Ronne Ice Shelf

Ellsworth Land

Krill

Emperor penguins

Blue whale

Ice-breaker

Antarctic Circle

Southern Ocean

118

Who was the first person to reach the South Pole?

Right whale

Southern Ocean

Antarctic science

The only people who live in Antarctica are scientists. They use huge balloons to study the climate on Antarctica.

Weather balloon.

Dronning Maud Land

Molodezhnaya Station (Russian Federation)

Survey plane

Adélie penguins

Antarctica

Princess Elizabeth Land

Amundsen-Scott Station (USA), South Pole

SOUTH POLE

Snow mobile

Elephant seal

Vostok Station (Russian Federation)

Antarctic Mountains

Casey Base (Australia)

oss Ice Shelf

McMurdo Air Station (USA)

oss Sea

Sno-cat

Dumont d'Urville (France)

Snow petrel

Killer whale

Life in the freezer

Antarctica is so cold that it freezes your breath into icicles around your mouth. People have to cover up in lots of very warm clothes.

Icicles from breath.

The Norwegian explorer Roald Amundsen, in 1911.

Flags of the World

NORTH AND SOUTH AMERICA

Canada	United States of America	Mexico	Guatemala	Belize	Honduras	El Salvador	Nicaragua
St Kitts and Nevis	Dominica	St Lucia	St Vincent and The Grenadines	Barbados	Grenada	Trinidad and Tobago	Venezuela

AFRICA

Argentina	Paraguay	Uruguay	Morocco	Algeria	Tunisia	Libya	Egypt
Guinea-Bissau	Guinea	Sierra Leone	Liberia	Ivory Coast	Burkina	Ghana	Togo
Sao Tome and Principe	Gabon	Congo	Democratic Republic of Congo	Uganda	Rwanda	Burundi	Kenya

EUROPE

Swaziland	South Africa	Lesotho	Madagascar	Comoros	Cape Verde	Iceland	Norway
France	Monaco	Germany	Austria	Switzerland	Liechtenstein	Spain	Andorra
Ukraine	Moldova	Poland	Czech Republic	Slovakia	Hungary	Slovenia	Croatia

RUSSIA AND CENTRAL ASIA

Cyprus	Russian Federation	Georgia	Azerbaijan	Armenia	Kazakhstan	Uzbekistan	Turkmenistan
Iraq	Kuwait	Saudi Arabia	Bahrain	Qatar	United Arab Emirates	Oman	Yemen
Vietnam	Cambodia	Philippines	Malaysia	Singapore	Brunei	Indonesia	East Timor

AUSTRALIA AND THE PACIFIC

Maldives	Mauritius	Seychelles	Australia	New Zealand	Palau	Micronesia	Marshall Islands

Which is the only country that doesn't have a rectangular flag?

There are 196 countries in the world. Each has its own flag.

Costa Rica — Panama — Bahamas — Cuba — Jamaica — Haiti — Dominican Republic — Antigua & Barbuda

Colombia — Guyana — Surinam — Ecuador — Peru — Brazil — Bolivia — Chile

Mauritania — Mali — Niger — Chad — Sudan — Southern Sudan — Eritrea — Senegal — Gambia

Benin — Nigeria — Cameroon — Central African Republic — Ethiopia — Djibouti — Somalia — Equatorial Guinea

Tanzania — Angola — Zambia — Malawi — Mozambique — Namibia — Botswana — Zimbabwe

Sweden — Finland — Denmark — United Kingdom — Ireland — Netherlands — Belgium — Luxembourg

Portugal — Italy — San Marino — Vatican City — Malta — Estonia — Latvia — Lithuania — Belarus

Romania — Bosnia & Herzegovina — Kosovo — Montenegro — Serbia — Bulgaria — Macedonia — Albania — Greece

ASIA

Kyrgyzstan — Tajikistan — Turkey — Iran — Lebanon — Syria — Israel — Jordan

Afghanistan — Pakistan — India — Bangladesh — Sri Lanka — Myanmar — Laos — Thailand

Papua New Guinea — Mongolia — China — Nepal — Bhutan — North Korea — South Korea — Taiwan — Japan

Nauru — Kiribati — Solomon Islands — Tuvalu — Samoa — Vanuatu — Fiji — Tonga

Index

Reference Section

Acknowledgements

Dorling Kindersley would like to thank:

Andrew O'Brien for additional digital artworks; Chris Bernstein for compiling the index; Lisa Magloff for editorial assistance and proof reading; Abbie Collinson and Sadie Thomas for design assistance; Pilar Morales for DTP assistance; Simon Mumford for DK cartography; Karl Stange, Gemma Woodward, and Sarah Mills for DK Picture Library research

Picture credits

Dorling Kindersley would like to thank the following for their kind permission to reproduce their photographs :
(Key: a = above; b = below; c = centre; l = left; r = right; t = top)

Action Plus: Eric Bretagnon/DPPI 78br; Glyn Kirk 116cbr; **Agence France Presse:** 76cb, 90cla; 49cal; **alamy.com:** Bryan and Cherry Alexander 117r; Jon Arnold Images 54tl, 77cal; Peter Bowater 111cra; Jon Bower 104l; Rosemary Calvert 85cra; Brandon Cole Marine Photography 11ca; Alan Copson Pictures 50t; Stephen Coyne 78cla; Chad Ehlers 9r; foodfolio 71cla; Robert Francis 87c; Ken Gillham 76cbl; Robert Harding World Imagery 77cbr, 86tr; Esa Hiltula 44tcr; Frank Krahmer 87br; Andre Jenny 9bl; Brian Lawrence 67tr; Pete Oxford / Steve Bloom Images 8; Pictor International 105b, 115tr; Wolfgang Pölzer 11r; Rolf Richardson 76cbr; Sami Sarkis71tr; Paul Springett 2-3; J Stock 2-3; Petr Svarc 104bc; A. T. Willett 9tl; **Bryan And Cherry Alexander Photography:** 14-15, 14car, 15tl, 15car, 16bl, 41cr, 85cla, 85ca; 88br; 88; © **A.M.P.A.S ®:** Oscar statuette is the registered trademark and copyrighted property of the Academy of Motion Arts and Sciences 25cb; **Ardea London Ltd:** 21cbl, 26cra, 72ca, 79cla; **Andrew Butler:** 110tr; **Corbis:** 54clb, 91cr, 103car; AFP 45tr; O. Alamany & E. Vicens 74l; Paul Almasy 16cb, 17tr, 37tl, 63clb, 80cr, 85cl, 99cal; James L. Amos 13tr; Archivo Iconografico, S.A. 55tr, 57c; Tony Arruza 20bl, 49cbr; Yann Arthus-Bertrand 91cbl, 110cra; Craig Aurness 91br; Roger Ball 61cbl; Dave Bartruff 63cl, 108bc; Tom Bean 26ca; Morton Beebe 62-63; Annebicque Bernard/ Sygma 56cr; Bettmann 48bcl, 70tr, 71c, 118bl, 118cbl; Jonathan Blair 41bcl; Georgina Bowater 59cl, 91c; Tom Brakefield 1cr, 27bc, 27br, 57bl, 101r; Jan Butchofsky-Houser 77cra; Michelle Chaplow 64cbr; L. Clarke 113cb; Lloyd Cluff 42br; Dean Conger 79br, 98cra, 99cla; Richard Cummins 49car; Tim Davis 118tl, 119ca; Carlos Dominguez 44bc; Robert Dowling 60c; Duomo 46tr; Ric Ergenbright 84br; Macduff Everton 101t; Eye Ubiquitous 16tc, 17cra, 21clb, 81cb, 91bc, 94cal; 96l, 116c; Sandy Felsenthal 1ca, 26ca; Owen Franken 59cr, 99clb; Michael Freeman 80cra, 94cra, 108c; Fukuhara, Inc. 109cl; Raymond Gehman 17bl; Todd A. Gipstein 68ca; Tim Graham/Sygma 50b; Annie Griffiths Belt 23tl; Darrell Gulin 26cal; Dan Guravich 84br; Paul Hardy 54cb, 92br; Blaine Harrington III 34b; Jason Hawkes 49cbr; Dallas and John Heaton 6crb, 47r, 61c, 72bc, 73cal, 102bl, 114bl; Chris Hellier 90b, 91tl; Robert Holmes 24ca; Jeremy Horner 94tr, 100c, 101bl; 102crb; Dave G. Houser 47cl, 92l, 100-101; Peter Johnson 41ca, 116br; Dewitt Jones 51bc; Hekimian Julien 51bl; Ray Juno 61r; Wolfgang Kaehler 61clb, 63crb, 85cb, 88l, 116cb, 119cb; Steve Kaufman 20crb, 108cal; Richard Klune 55cr; Frank Lane Picture Agency 98cb, 99cla; Maurizio Lanini 61car; Lester Lefkowits 1c, Alain Le Garsmeur 103cal; Danny Lehman 90tr; Charles & Josette Lenars 99cbr; Liu Liqun 103cl; Chris Lisle 45c;

Massimo Listri 60cra; Yang Liu 103cb; Craig Lovell 72bc, 73cb, 109cbl; Christophe Loviny 98ca; Renee Lynn 85cra; William Manning 21tl; James Marshall 33tl; Dennis Marsico 117bl; Francis G. Mayer 56crb; Jim McDonald 77cbl; Wally McNamee 25ca, 78b; John McPherson 51r; Milepost 92 _/ Colin Garratt 49tr, 57tl; Sally A. Morgan/ Ecoscene 57tc; Warren Morgan 116tr; Christopher J. Morris 65cl; Francesc Muntada 72cal; Anthony Nex 37ca; Michael Nicholson 77c; Alain Nogues/ Sygma 56crb; Richard T. Nowitz 33cbl; Elizabeth Opalenik 38-39; Charles O'Rear 39cla, 82cr; Diego Lezama Orezzoli 30cra; Van Parys 53cla; Caroline Penn 38tr, 89tl; Caron Philippe 49br; Giraud Philippe 36tr; Amet Jean Pierre 46cra; Michael Pole 116cr; Rick Price 119cal; Carl & Ann Purcell 42br, 80cbr; Jose Fuste Raga 60cb, 72cbl; Steve Raymer 76cbr; Reuter Raymond 53ca; Carmen Redondo 36cbl, 73cal; Roger Ressmeyer 23cra, 49car, 84cb, 110bl; Hans Georg Roth 67br; Arthur Rothstein 80cbl; Galen Rowell 1cr, 30bc, 119cl, 119c, 119cbl; Kevin Schafer 47cla; Alan Schein Photography 91crb; Houston Scott 109tl; Sean Sexton Collection 71ca; Shepard Sherbell/ SABA 119tr; Ariel Skelley 24-25; Douglas Slone 22tr; Paul A. Souders 45cbl, 112cbl, 117cl; Hubert Stadler 35tr, 35clb; Mark L Stephenson 70b; David Stoecklein 61car; Vince Streano 68tc; Keren Su 89clb, 98ca, 102cla, 103tc; Liba Taylor 73cal; Tim Thompson 75r, 83cbl; Roger Tidman 36cbr, 118ca; David Turnley 85bl, 87bl; Peter Turnley 60cl, 78tr, 91ca; Vanni Archive 81r; Brian A. Vikander 102cr, 107c; Uwe Walz 60ca; Patrick Ward 49cla, 115cr, 116l; Karl Weatherly 61tc; Robert Weight/ Ecoscene 119cla; K.M. Westermann 36cb; Nik Wheeler 56tr, 91cal, 91tcl; Adam Woolfitt 61tcl; Michael S. Yamashita 98cr, 105tl; Jim Zuckerman 28r, 38bl, 56bl, 100l; **Tim Daly:** 49cal; **Philip Dowell:** 30cbr, 32cbl; **Alistair Duncan:** 36tcr, 91cl; **Gables Travels:** 36br, 37clb, 94c, 102cb, 102cbr; **Getty Images:** 20crb, 21cl, 22tl, 22cr, 30cbl, 49tc, 55, 65car, 109cl; Peter Adams 94crb; Yves Debay 37bc; Guido Alberto Rossi 28l, 68cr; Jon Arnold 49car; Brian Bahr 25br; Daryl Balfour 37tl; James Balog 15cr; Brett Baunton 73br; Josef Beck 63ca; Benelux Press 82; John Callahan 10-11; David Cannon 31cla; Anthony Cassidy 113cb; Flip Chalfant 21c; China Tourism Press 104cra, 105tr; Geoffrey Clifford 35tl; Color Day Production 82cla; Cosmo Condina 29clb; Joe Cornish 56car; Doug Corrance 48crb; Joseph Devenney 27ca; Nicholas DeVore 40cla; Antony Edwards 48tr,59r; Michael Freeman 1car, 27cl; Robert Frerck 26tl; Stephen Frink 21br, 64cal; Paul Harris 12bc; David Kjaer 17cr; Jerry Kobalenko 79r; Hideo Kurihara 117cla; Yann Layma 104crb; Frans Lemmens 37ca, 52cal; Will & Deni McIntyre 27cr; Alan Majchrowicz 8br; Barbara Maurer 92r; Ted Mead 114-115; NASA 43tr; Donald Nausbaum 33r; James Nelson 29cr; Mike Powell 19tc, 59bl; Martin Puddy 95r; Terje Rakke 45clb; John R. Ramey 45bcl; Edwin Remsberg 1car; Galen Rowell 27cra; Thomas Schmitt 112ca; Herb Schmitz 116bl; Felix St. Clair Renard 62bl; Space Frontiers 89r; James Strachan 42l; David Sutherland 84cal, 86l; Pete Turner 20cra; Alvis Upitis 44tr; Art Wolfe 9cl, 69c, 69cbl; Jeremy Woodhouse 53r; **Glasgow Museum:** 92cb, 97tr; **Robert Harding Picture**

Library: 18br, 31cl; C Bowman 52cbr, 80ca; Robert Frerck 32l; N. Hangay 107tl; R Harding 3r, 19r, 94bcr; Gavin Hellier 55tl; D.Jacobs 113cla; David Lomax 46b; A.Neville 93ca; P Robinson 80cbr; Silvestris 63cla; Paul Van Riel 110; A Woolfitt 83tc; A Wright 94cb; **HB Oktoberfest Beer:** 61c; **Sean Hunter:** 1caa, 20cl, 22-23b; 68cb, 69cbl; © FMGB Guggenheim Bilbao Museoa 2003. All rights reserved. Total or partial reproduction is prohibited. 65tl; **Hutchison Library:** 96-97; David Brincombe 7c, 40; Jon Burbank 110-111; Andrew Eames 84ca, 118crb; Bernard Gerard 93r; Patricio Goycoo 107br; Bernard Regent 46clb, 66tr; Isabella Tree 13cb; **Images Of Africa Photobank:** David Keith Jones 37cla; **ImageState/Pictor:** 27cl; 32cr, 58tr, 69cl, 94cbr, 99cra, 109cr, 109cbl, 112cr, 115cl; Randa Bishop 109cla; Douglas David Seifert 26cl; Ethel Davies 95clb; **Impact Photos:** Christophe Bluntzer 107cl; **INAH:** 1cc 26cr, 27clb, 28-29; **Katz/FSP:** Liaison 20bcl; **Barnaba Kindersley:** 17cla, 68cbr, 102cra; **Nicolas Lewis:** 39cr; **Lonely Planet Images:** Rhonda Gutenberg 80car; Crc Pershouse 76ca, 76cbr; Tony Wheeler 81c; **Marwell Zoological Park:** 44c; **Leon Mead:** 114ca; **Tracy Morgan:** 49cal; **Mountain Camera/John Cleare:** 107tr; **David Murray & Jules Selmes:** 31bl, 65c, 69tl 99cbl, 111br; **Museo Archeologico Nazionale di Napoli:** 69cal; **NASA:** Finley Holiday Films 1car, 21crb; C. Mayhew & R. Simmon 4bl; **National Maritime Museum:** 103crb; **National Trust Authority:** 48cr; **Natural History Museum:** 2tr, 26cc 36cr, 85c, 98cr, 103cbr, 109cl, 113cl; **Nature Picture Library:** Ingo Arndt 1cbr, 31br; Martin Dohrn 31cl; Vincent Munier 108tl; Peter Oxford 106tr; TJ Rich 85cbl; Anup Shah 37r; Lynn M. Stone 94cl; **Mrs C.P. Neeson, Plaxtol, Kent/Campanero XIV:** 65cbl; **N.H.P.A.:** A.N.TN 112clb; Bill Coster 85tl; Stephen Dalton 32cla; Daniel Heuclin 41cla; B Jones & M Shimlock 112clb; Peter Pickford 32-33; Andy Rouse 96- Kevin Schafer 34tr; Norbert Wu 10bl; **Odds Farm Park:** 48c; Oxford Scientific Films: David Fleetham 112clb; Tom Leach 63cla; Colin Monteath 95c; Mike Powles 44cb; **Amit Pasricha/Avinash Pasricha:** 97tl; **Pictures Colour Library:** 46l; Charles Bowman 44cbr George Hunter 16br;Edmund Nagele 49cb; **Pitt Rivers Museum:** 88tr; **Popperfoto:** 87cb; China Photo/ Reuters 89cal; Petr Josek/ Reuters 83br; **Powerstock:** 25tr, 54cr, 54-55, 109cl; J.Beck 98c; Werner Otto 63crar Alan Wycheck 65bl; **Antony Pozner, Hendon Way Motors:** 68c, 71bc; **Magnus Rew:** 91cla; **Royal British Columbia Museum, Victoria, Canada:** 77cbl, 77bcr **Guy Ryecart:** 69tl; **Science Photo Library:** Bernard Edmaier 12 background; Simon Fraser 14-15; Chris Madeley 14tc; David Vaughan 14car; **Seapics.com:** Doug Perrine 10-11; Neil Setchfield: 1ca, 20clb; **Still Pictures:** 44crb; Mark Edwards 114tr; Nicolas Granier 42tr; Sergio Hanquet 113r; Roger de la Harpe 7cr, 41r; Thomas Kelly 106br; Andre Maslennikov 47tc; Andrea Riedmiller 61cbr; **Stanislav Tereba/Olympia:** 72crb, 74-75; **Weymouth Sea Life Centre:** 45c, 112bl; **Wor Pictures:** 1br, 35br, 44ca, 58l, 63tl, 66cr, 66l, 69br, 74cra, 74crb, 75cl, 83cla, 93tl, 93clb, 98bl, 110-111; **Jerry Young:** 12crb, 13c, 15tr, 26cra, 36cra, 37cl, 45tr 47cla, 69tcl, 80cal, 85cal, 112car.